# The Mind of Christ

*Claude V. King*

## LEADER'S GUIDE

Scripture quotations marked (NIV) are from the Holy Bible,
*New International Version,* copyright © 1973, 1978, 1984 by International Bible Society.
Scripture quotations marked (NASB) are from the *New American Standard Bible.*
© The Lockman Foundation, 1960, 1962, 1963, 1968, 1971, 1972, 1973, 1975, 1977. Used by permission.

ISBN: 0-8054-9869-9
Dewey Decimal Classification: 248.4
Subject Heading: CHRISTIAN LIFE—STUDY AND TEACHING

*Printed in the United States of America.*

Note: Page numbers identified in this Leader's Guide will be followed by LG.
Unless otherwise noted, all other page references refer to pages in
*The Mind of Christ Member's Book* (LIFE course).

LifeWay Press
127 Ninth Avenue, North
Nashville, Tennessee 37234

# THE MIND OF CHRIST
## CONTENTS

*Having loved his own…
he now showed them the
full extent of his love.*

*—John 13:1, NIV*

The night before His crucifixion, Jesus ate His last meal with His beloved disciples. John tells us: "Jesus knew that the time had come for him to leave this world and go to the Father. Having loved his own who were in the world, he now showed them the full extent of his love" (John 13:1, NIV). When Jesus went to the cross, He forever demonstrated the fullest dimensions of God's love for us. Jesus died so that we might have life in Him for eternity.

One day we, too, will sit down to dine with Jesus. We will sit down with Him at the marriage supper of the Lamb. The Bride (the church) will be forever wed to her Bridegroom (Jesus). Knowing the depth of the love Jesus has for us draws us into the most intimate love relationship with Him. *The Mind of Christ* is about a love relationship where we allow Christ to live in us and through us, where we become like Him. The Father is calling His people to that kind of love relationship with His Son Jesus.

On July 18, 1989, T. W. Hunt, Henry Blackaby, Avery Willis, and I were training prayer leaders in North Carolina. T. W. began teaching about the importance of united prayer. Soon into his lecture, he said, "I don't know why, but I think I need to share something with you." He told us about his lifelong sense that Christ was preparing to return soon to take away His bride.

T. W. told us what the Lord did to teach him about the mind of Christ. He told us about his wife Laverne being diagnosed with breast cancer. Under the stress of seeing her suffer with the radiation and chemotherapy, he went into his office one day and locked the door behind him. Feeling helpless and broken, he fell to the floor, emotionally shattered. The Lord met him there.

T. W. sensed the Lord saying, "You teach *The Mind of Christ,* but there is something about My mind that you do not know. I knew you could not possibly understand unless I brought you through this experience. You see, you are broken and hurting because your bride Laverne is very sick. I, too, have a bride and she is very sick—sin sick. I knew that you couldn't possibly understand the heartache I feel without my allowing you to experience a heartache for your bride." T. W. knew that the Scripture indicates the Bride—the church—will make herself ready for the marriage supper with the Lamb (see Rev. 19:7). There on the floor in his office, he sensed the Lord calling him to help the bride get ready—to purify herself.

*The Mind of Christ* fits into what God is doing. God is calling His people to return to Him for cleansing and revival. We need to allow the Lord Jesus to renew our minds to be like the mind of Christ Himself. We need to be filled with His Holy Spirit and fully surrendered to His lordship.

Some time ago I talked with a pastor in Nashville, Tennessee. He said the Lord gave him a parable of the bride. Consider a human bride on her wedding day. Only hours before the wedding, she looks nothing like a bride. But with the wedding approaching, the bride quickens her pace. She enlists the help of others as she gets ready. In just a short time, the preparation is completed. When the wedding march begins to play, she is adorned in pure white ready to meet her bridegroom.

The church is far from looking like a pure bride ready to meet her Bridegroom—the Lord Jesus. But when the church realizes the time for the wedding is drawing near, she WILL make herself ready. We pray that these are the days when the bride will purify herself for her wedding day. May *The Mind of Christ* be part of the preparation. Maranatha! Come Lord Jesus.

Claude V. King
Murfreesboro, Tennessee
April 1994

This *Leader's Guide* primarily is for use by the person who facilitates a small-group study of *The Mind of Christ* LIFE course. If your church plans to offer a variety of approaches to studying *The Mind of Christ*, the person coordinating these approaches also will find this guide helpful. If you fit one of those two descriptions, this guide is for you. If you are not a pastor and your pastor is not involved directly in leading a group study, you may want to provide him a copy so he can become familiar with the various approaches to offering *The Mind of Christ* in your church.

## Overview

Paul said, "Let this mind be in you, which was also in Christ Jesus" (Phil. 2:5). *The Mind of Christ* resources help believers keep that command. In Luke 17:21 Jesus said, "the kingdom of God is within you." Jesus emphasized that the kingdom of God does not come with outward observance, but by an inner working that is not seen. That directs us to the mind, the area where God wants to work. The changes that God brings in a believer's life are secret and inward, but they will bear fruit that will be visible in life and lifestyle. When church leaders help members develop the mind of Christ, the body of Christ can function the way God intended to reveal His Son to a watching world. *The Mind of Christ* resources will help you lead members of your church to develop the mind of Christ under the leadership and empowering of the Holy Spirit.

## The Hymn

*The Mind of Christ* resources examine the poem in Philippians 2:5-11. This poem was actually a hymn and probably was sung during times of worship in the early church. The hymn has been divided into six parts for this study:

### Philippians 2:5-11

Part 1: Christ's Freedom

Part 2: Christ's Lifestyle

Part 3: Christ's Servanthood

Part 4: Christ's Humanity

Part 5: Christ's Holiness and Love

Part 6: Christ's Name

As members study each part of this hymn, they will understand how God wants to work to transform them into the image of His Son Jesus.

## The Resources

A variety of resources that support different approaches to studying *The Mind of Christ* will allow you to help people at all stages of maturity, levels of commitment, and learning styles. Information on the approaches will come later in this section.

• *The Mind of Christ Leader's Guide* by Claude V. King (7200-20)—This 64-page guide you are reading provides administrative guidelines, small-group learning activities, and supplementary teaching aids for church leaders who facilitate the use of *The Mind of Christ* resources or who lead small groups studying *The Mind of Christ Member's Book*.

• *The Mind of Christ Member's Book* by T. W. Hunt and Claude V. King (7200-19)—A 224-page self-paced interactive study of the mind of Christ. The 12 units serve as an introduction to using the learning helps for a lifelong process of developing the mind of Christ. Six pages of memory aids are included. This LIFE course is for individual study and is intended to be accompanied by weekly small-group learning sessions described later in this *Leader's Guide*.

• *The Mind of Christ Conference Video Series* (7700-20)—Three 120-minute videotapes featuring T. W. Hunt in a church conference setting and in small-group dialogue with three conference participants. These conference videos can be used individually or in small and large groups. The conference can be spread over a 12-week period or conducted over a concentrated two- or three-day period. A copy of the *Listening Guide* (listed separately below) is included.

• *The Mind of Christ Worship Video Series* (7700-21)—Two 60-minute video messages featuring T. W. Hunt detailing Christ's experiences during the crucifixion and resurrection. These two messages can be used with *The Mind of Christ Conference Video Series*, the LIFE course, or they also can stand alone for use in corporate worship experiences.

• *The Mind of Christ Audiocassettes* (7700-22)— Audio messages from *The Mind of Christ* conference by T. W. Hunt on eight 60-minute audiocassettes with one copy of the *Listening Guide* (listed separately below). The audiocassettes are for individual listening and study.

• *The Mind of Christ Listening Guide* (7200-21)—A 32-page book that serves as a listening and viewing guide for participants who use the Conference Video Series and/or the Audiocassettes. Each individual or participant in a group will need a copy for notes and future study and application.

• *The Mind of Christ Leader's Kit* (7700-11)—Includes one copy of each resource listed above.

• *The Mind of Christ* by T. W. Hunt (Broadman & Holman, 4211-66)—A book with a thorough biblical and theological treatment of the mind of Christ including detailed chapters on the crucifixion and resurrection. This book is for individual reading and study.

## Size of Groups for Effective Learning

Jesus preached to large crowds, but He did most of His discipleship training with a group of 12 men. Jesus trained more intimately three of His disciples (Peter, James, and John) who would be key leaders in the New Testament church. With *The Mind of Christ* resources, you can provide large-group learning experiences as well as learning in a small-group setting.

A large-group setting can reach more people quicker but only provides a beginning level of learning. You will want to provide a learning environment in which God can do His best work in the lives of members. For God to do a deeper work, individuals need to be in a small group where they can ask questions, share personal experiences, encourage one another toward love and good deeds (see Heb. 10:24), and pray intimately with brothers and sisters in Christ. They need to be in a group where they will be more of a participant than a spectator.

## The Approaches

Because having the mind of Christ is essential for every believer, we recommend that you consider a variety of approaches that can help people at varied stages of maturity, levels of commitment, and with learning styles. These approaches serve as an introduction to a lifelong process as God continually renews the minds and lives of Christians to reflect the image of His Son Jesus. Some members will benefit from participating in several or perhaps all of these approaches. With each approach, God works in different ways to orient more thoroughly a person to Himself. By offering different approaches in your church, you will introduce more of your members to the message.

☙ **Individual Study.** Individuals can study any of the resources at their own pace. They can either (1) read the Broadman & Holman book, (2) listen to the audiocassettes, (3) watch the videotapes, or (4) study the LIFE course member's book. Making the resources available in the church media library and/or for sale to members will encourage individual study. Recommend that individuals consider participating in some group format to benefit from the encouragement and interaction with other believers.

☙ **Video Conference.** For years T. W. Hunt has led weekend conferences on *The Mind of Christ* in churches across the country. Now you can have Dr. Hunt in your church leading the conference by video. You are not limited, however, by his schedule. You can conduct the conference on a weekend, weekdays, week nights, spread it out over 12 weeks, or do all of the above! Let Dr. Hunt do the teaching and preaching on the video series during the evening worship services. Many people have found that one time through is not enough, so you can repeat the conference as often as you choose at your convenience. Members who miss a session can make it up by checking out the videos for home viewing. The video conference will take at least eight hours and includes both the Conference Video Series (6 hours) and the Worship Video Series (2 hours). Additional time will permit your group to discuss and process what they experience on the videotape. Then group members can help each other in making application to their lives. A possible schedule might be:

• Singing and Review/Overview—10 minutes

• Video Viewing—30 minutes

• Video Discussion/Response—15 minutes

• Closure/Invitation—5 minutes

🔖 **Individual and Small-Group Study Combination.** The LIFE course *Member's Book* and this *Leader's Guide* are for a combination of individual study with a small-group session once each week. This combination of more in-depth study and small-group interaction will enhance learning and contribute to greater application of the material. With this approach, you will need a small group for each eight to ten participants. If you have more than ten persons interested in the course, provide multiple groups in order to create the best possible learning environment. If you do not have sufficient leaders, start a waiting list for the next group. In the meantime, begin training new leaders within the group or groups you currently have. The remainder of this *Leader's Guide* provides information on leading this approach.

Rather than choosing one approach, consider offering *The Mind of Christ* in as many ways as possible. You will be more likely to encourage everyone to participate in the study when they can choose their learning approach. Promotion masters are provides on pages 62-64 LG for use in promoting the LIFE course, video conference series, and worship video series.

Remember, interaction with other believers allows God to work through different members of the body of Christ to bring about change in the body. Encourage all church members to study *The Mind of Christ*.

---

**Summary of Approaches in Offering**
*The Mind of Christ*

**LIFE Course**
(Interactive personal study with small-group meetings)
• Member's Book
• Leader's Guide
• Worship Video Series (optional)

**Video Conference**
(Video-based group study)
• Conference Video Series
• Worship Video Series
• Leader's Guide
• Listening Guide

**Audiocassette Series**
(Audio-based personal study)
• Audiocassette Series
• Listening Guide

**Book Study**
(Personal study)
• *The Mind of Christ* (Broadman & Holman book)

**Worship Experience**
(Corporate worship service)
• Worship Video Series
• Leader's Guide

**The Lay Institute For Equipping**

One approach to *The Mind of Christ* is a course in the Lay Institute For Equipping or LIFE. LIFE is an educational system designed to provide quality Christian education to laypersons in the areas of discipleship, leadership, and ministry. All LIFE courses have common characteristics. These apply to *The Mind of Christ* LIFE course.

• Participants interact with a self-paced workbook (the member's book) for 30 to 60 minutes each day and complete life-related learning activities.

• Participants meet for a one- to two-hour small-group session each week.

• The course leader (or facilitator) guides group members to reflect on and discuss what they have studied during the week and then make practical application of the study to everyday life. This small group becomes a base of support for participants as they help each other understand and apply the Scriptures to life.

• Most LIFE courses have optional videotapes that provide additional content and learning experiences. *The Mind of Christ Conference Video Series* is different in that the video series stands alone as a seminar approach. Also, the order of the material is not the same. The tapes do not go into the same depth of study or provide the practical lifelong helps that are included in the printed material. They will, however, provide an opportunity to hear T. W. Hunt share personal experiences, teach on each subject, and answer questions that may arise in the minds of participants.

*The Mind of Christ Worship Video Series* includes presentations by T. W. Hunt on the crucifixion and resurrection. These two presentations can be a significant part of the LIFE course. They deal with subject matter communicated better through video than in print. These presentations are recommended in units 11 and 12 of the LIFE course.

• Individuals may receive a Church Study Course diploma for studying *The Mind of Christ* in one of three ways:

  • *The Mind of Christ* (courses 03-398 through 03-403)

  • *The Mind of Christ Conference Video Series* (courses 03-409 through 03-414)

  • *The Mind of Christ Audiocassette Series* (courses 03-415 through 03-420)

The same diploma will be issued for either of three ways to study *The Mind of Christ*. However, a seal indicating the form of study will be issued to attach to the diploma. For example, when completing the LIFE course, a diploma with a LIFE seal will be issued. Use the appropriate Form 725 to indicate the proper form of study. The LIFE form is found in the *Member's Book*. The Conference Video Series and Audiocassette Series forms are found in the *Listening Guide*.

*The Mind of Christ* and other LIFE courses are offered through the discipleship program of a church. If your church does not have a regular training program, you can still offer the course. In fact, some churches are using LIFE courses to start or revitalize their training of disciples. If you would like to learn more about the Lay Institute For Equipping and other LIFE courses request a catalog from: LIFE (MSN 151); 127 Ninth Avenue, North; Nashville, TN 37234.

**Getting Started**

The more familiar you are with the message and the resources of *The Mind of Christ*, the better prepared you will be to use this guide with the LIFE-course approach. Complete the following activities to familiarize yourself with the LIFE course.

• In *The Mind of Christ Member's Book:*

❑ Read the Preface and the Introduction (pp. 6-10).

❑ Read about the Disciple's Cross on the inside back cover to get an overview of LIFE.

❏ Read the table of contents (pp. 3-4) to get an overall view of the course.

❏ Read through the Lifelong Helps section (pp. 186-221) to get an idea of the learning aids available.

❏ Look at the cards in the back of the book to see the memory aids that can be used for review.

• In this *Leader's Guide* (LG):

❏ Read the table of contents (p. 3 LG) and scan through this guide to familiarize yourself with the learning aids.

❏ Read the remainder of this section and decide how you will conduct the study.

☙ **Decide when and where groups will meet.** We recommend one- to two-hour small-group sessions. One hour is a minimum. Groups should allow two hours if they intend to deal fully with Dr. Hunt's principles. Some groups may prefer to double the number of weeks and spend one hour each week on one half the recommended content for each unit.

Groups may meet at the church, in homes, community centers, a workplace, or other locations convenient to members. You may want to offer group studies at a variety of times and locations so more people will be able to participate. Consider these options:

• **Sunday evenings**

–Begin one to two hours before evening worship.

–Meet in small groups before worship to process what members have learned during their study of the *Member's Book*.

• **Weekdays**

–Meet at church at a convenient time to those involved. For instance, a senior adult group might meet before or after noon once a week and eat a sack lunch together in conjunction with their small-group study.

–Meet in homes at a convenient time to those involved. Homes often provide a quiet and more informal atmosphere for sharing and praying. Be sure to set guidelines about leaving times, so the group does not wear out its welcome.

–At the workplace. Some employees may want to meet before or after work once a week at their workplace provided their employer approves. Others may decide to bring lunch and spend two lunch breaks together each week.

☙ **Develop a time schedule.** A typical weekly session might look like this. Definitions of each segment are provided later in this section.

---

### Small-group Study: One Hour/Two Hours

• Hearing What the Spirit Is Saying (as members arrive)

• Magnifying the Lord and Exalting His Name (5/10 minutes)

• Transforming by the Word (15/30 minutes)

• Stimulating to Love and Good Deeds (20/40 minutes)

• Preparing the Bride for Her Bridegroom (5/10 minutes)

• Praying for One Another (10/20 minutes)

• Closing the Session (5/10 minutes)

---

An option is to kick off the study with a weekend video conference using *The Mind of Christ Conference Video Series*. The LIFE course would begin shortly thereafter for interested participants using the small-group agenda for the weekly sessions.

☙ **Decide on the number of groups needed.** Work with your pastor, discipleship director, minister of education, or other church leaders to determine how many individuals in your church want to study this course at this time. Adults who have surrendered their lives to Jesus Christ as Lord and Savior will benefit from this study. Survey your church members to determine the number of persons interested in a study to develop the mind of Christ. You may want to publicize the study using announcements in your church publications (see Promotion Masters, pp. 62-64 LG). Remember that you will need one group for every 10 members.

🔊 **Enlist leaders.** Each group will need a separate leader. Pastor, you may want to lead the first group and train eight to ten persons to provide leadership for future groups. If you need more leaders, you may want to take two or more groups through the course at different times during the week. Leading the first group will demonstrate your belief in what *The Mind of Christ* is about. It also will be enriching and helpful in your walk with the Lord. If you are unable to lead the first group, enlist another church staff member or lay leader.

Pray that God will help you identify those persons He wants to lead the groups. These leaders should be spiritually growing Christians and active church members. Leaders should have teachable spirits, the ability to relate well to people, a commitment to keep information private, and a willingness to spend the time necessary to prepare for the sessions. Also look for people who possess skills for leading small-group learning activities. Do *not* select someone who is having spiritual, marital, or physical difficulties that could hinder their effectiveness.

If you do not have enough leaders (maximum of 10 members per group) to accommodate all those who want to participate, enlist additional leaders from those who plan to participate. However, use the same criteria for all leaders. If you don't have qualified leaders, start a waiting list and encourage members to pray that God will call out additional leaders. Some leaders might be willing to lead a second group at a different time during the week since little additional preparation would be required.

🔊 **Enlist participants.** Invite to the introductory session church leaders and other prospective participants. Use the promotion master on page 62 LG in church newsletters, as a bulletin insert, or enlarge it and use it as a poster.

The introductory session provides enough information for persons to decide whether to participate in the study. At the end of the session, give those present an opportunity to sign up for the course. If persons are unwilling to make a commitment to individual and group study, encourage them not to participate at this time. Remind them of the other opportunities to study *The Mind of Christ* through the video and audio-cassette approaches.

🔊 **Order resources.** Resources should be ordered for the course eight to ten weeks prior to the introductory session. Although processing and shipping your order may take less time, leaders need time to prepare for the introductory session and time to enlist participants. Though you may not enlist participants until later, you can estimate the quantity needed by ordering eight to ten copies of the *Member's Book* and one *Leader's Guide* for each small group you anticipate. Husbands and wives will each need a personal copy of the *Member's Book*. Resource descriptions and applications are on pages 7-8 LG.

Because the *The Mind of Christ Leader's Kit* (7700-11) includes one copy of each resource, you may want to purchase at least one kit for your church. Remember that the kit also includes the audiocassette and video conference series materials.

The recommended LIFE course resources include:

*The Mind of Christ Member's Book* (7200-19)

*The Mind of Christ Leader's Guide* (7200-20)

*The Mind of Christ Worship Video Series* (7700-21)

We encourage the use of the *Worship Video Series* with units 11 and 12. This is optional, but it will be a meaningful experience for participants.

---

Orders or order inquiries may be sent to Customer Service Center; 127 Ninth Avenue, North; Nashville, TN 37234, or you may call 1-800-458-2772. Telephone representatives are available between 8:00 a.m. and 5:30 p.m. Central Time, Monday–Friday. Western states may call 1-800-677-7797. The materials also are available nationwide at Baptist Book Stores and Lifeway Christian Stores.

---

🔊 **Set and collect fees.** We recommend that participants pay at least part of the cost of the materials so they make a commitment to the study with a financial investment. Announce the fee when you enlist participants so they will not be caught off guard or embarrassed at the introductory session. You may want to provide scholarships for those unable to participate due to lack of financial resources.

## How to Use This Guide for a Small-Group Study

This *Leader's Guide* assists you in preparing for and conducting the small-group learning sessions for a study of the LIFE course *The Mind of Christ*. Pages 19-47 LG provide step-by-step procedures for conducting an introductory session and 12 group sessions. Suggestions also are provided for using the two messages in *The Mind of Christ Worship Video Series*.

Each of the group sessions includes three parts:

- BEFORE THE SESSION—This section includes actions for you to complete prior to the group session. On page 17 LG you will find a Standard Before the Session list that will be referenced but not repeated each session. You may want to cut out this half page of your book and use it as a bookmark for this guide. The back side will have the Standard After the Session list.

- DURING THE SESSION—This section provides activities for you to use in conducting a one- to two-hour small-group session. You will find that the activities suggested will require more than one hour to process effectively. Don't get frustrated if you are limited to one-hour sessions. Adapt the activities and use the ones that are most helpful. The activities for the session follow a similar pattern each week. This simplifies your leadership role, but you should feel free to rearrange or adapt the sessions according to your group's needs.

- AFTER THE SESSION—This section guides you in evaluating the group session, your performance as a leader, and the needs of group members. This will help you improve your abilities to guide the group in their learning. As mentioned earlier, a Standard After the Session list is on page 18 LG. It can be cut out and used as a bookmark for quick reference at the end of each session.

Ballot boxes (❏) are provided in the Before the Session and After the Session sections for you to check as you complete each action. Sessions require a minimum of leader preparation so you can give yourself to prayer and personal spiritual preparation. If you adapt the lesson plans or create activities of your own, remember to secure any resources that are required for these activities.

Each week you are encouraged to think about your group members and identify one or more who may need a personal contact from you. Do not neglect this aspect of your ministry. Your primary assignment in this study is to help people develop the mind of Christ, not just teach knowledge about Christ.

## Seven Segments for DURING THE SESSION

Each session is divided into seven segments. The following segment descriptions will give you an overview of the process suggested for each session. The purpose is to help believers practice "being" the body of Christ. Because the sessions are designed to provide help for one- and two-hour sessions, you may find that they include far more than can be accomplished if you only have one hour. Regardless of time, God can work in every session to help members grow in Christlikeness. Evaluate the learning activities and determine which ones will be most helpful for the members of your group. Every group may be different in its needs. Adapt these plans for your group's needs.

The segments below have a suggested time frame beside them. The first number indicates a recommended time in minutes for a one-hour session. The second number indicates the time recommended for a two-hour session.

1. **Hearing What the Spirit is Saying (as members arrive).** "He that hath an ear, let him hear what the Spirit saith unto the churches" (Rev. 2:11). As members arrive before the session, guide them to review what God has been saying to them during the week. Ask members to identify a Scripture and a name of Christ that have been most meaningful this week. Ask them to identify and mark the issue or subject in which God seems to be working most actively to develop within them Christ's mind. Members will use these bits of information at various points in the session.

2. **Magnifying the Lord and Exalting His Name (5/10 minutes).** "O magnify the Lord with me, and let us exalt his name together" (Ps. 34:3). As you open each session in prayer, encourage members to worship God for Who He is and acknowledge Him for what He has done. Members may use the names of Christ to exalt His name together in prayer. Following the prayer time, give members a chance to share any ways

God may have revealed Himself this week through His names.

**3. Transforming by the Word (15/30 minutes).** "Christ also loved the church, and gave himself for it; that he might sanctify and cleanse it with the washing of water by the word, that he might present it to himself a glorious church, not having spot, or wrinkle, or any such thing; but that it should be holy and without blemish" (Eph. 5:25-27). Because the Scriptures reveal the nature, character, and standard for the mind and lifestyle of Christ, ask members to make two lists each week: (1) a list of things, actions, or attitudes identified in Scripture that need to be *cleansed from* one's mind and life, and (2) a list of things, actions, or attitudes that Scripture indicates need to be *incorporated into* one's mind and life. Ask members to review their memory verse for the week and share any Scripture that has been meaningful to them.

Because this activity may require more time than is allowed, you may want to try using it as an arrival activity. Let members begin the lists as they arrive. In this way you will be well along in the preparation of the lists by the starting time of the session. If you find, however, that members are consistently missing out on this activity, move it back to a time during the session.

**4. Stimulating One Another to Love and Good Deeds (20/40 minutes).** "Let us consider how to stimulate one another to love and good deeds" (Heb. 10:24, NASB). Because God did not intend for Christians to live their lives independently from the rest of the body, He made us dependent on one another. Use this period in each session to guide members in helping one another apply the truths of the Scriptures and the model of Christ to their own lives. This will be a time for discussion, testimony, encouragement, challenge, and accountability as members help one another respond to God's renewing process in their minds and lives.

Some people are far better at helping others than they are in receiving help themselves. For the body of Christ to function effectively, members need to learn to do both. If you see that some of your small group members tend to refuse help, you may want to take time to remind them about the importance of giving *and* receiving help. This is not to be a time for self-righteous people to "fix" everybody else. It is a time for humble servants to give and receive help.

**5. Preparing the Bride for Her Bridegroom (5/10 minutes).** "Let us be glad and rejoice, and give honour to him: for the marriage of the Lamb is come, and his wife hath made herself ready. And to her was granted that she should be arrayed in fine linen, clean and white: for the fine linen is the righteousness of saints. And he saith unto me, Write, Blessed are they which are called unto the marriage supper of the Lamb" (Rev. 19:7-9). As the marriage of Christ and His bride (the church) draws near, the bride must make herself ready. Christian churches must cleanse and purify themselves so they will be pleasing and acceptable to the Bridegroom. In each session, a Scripture will be examined that will help the bride prepare herself. Ask members to discuss and apply the Scripture to their lives, families, and church.

**6. Praying for One Another (10/20 minutes).** "Confess your faults one to another, and pray one for another, that ye may be healed. The effectual fervent prayer of a righteous man availeth much" (Jas. 5:16). Because God intends for a church to be a house of prayer (see Luke 19:46), members will take time each session sharing with one another in prayer. This will be an opportunity to share prayer requests for spiritual concerns; and confess faults, weaknesses, sins, struggles, and failures. But it will also be a time for praying fervently for one another for forgiveness, healing, encouragement, guidance, wisdom, knowledge, understanding, courage, strength, and faithfulness.

**7. Closing the Session (5/10 minutes).** At the conclusion of each session, summarize the questions that may still need answering and ask members to seek answers during the coming week. Take time to preview the coming unit and give any special instructions that may be helpful. Conclude the session in prayer.

### The Role of the Small-group Leader

You may have some feelings of inadequacy in leading a study about the mind of Christ. You may not feel like a knowledgeable person in the field. That is OK. Your role in this small-group study is not that of a teacher. You are a facilitator of a group-learning process. You will be helping members help each other by applying "Let us consider how to stimulate one another to love and good deeds" (Heb. 10:24, NASB).

If God has led you to accept this assignment, you can trust Him to equip and enable you to accomplish the task. You are an instrument through which God wants to do His work. Without God you can do nothing of Kingdom value. With Him you can move spiritual mountains. Depend on God and "pray without ceasing." Keep in mind that the Holy Spirit of Christ is present in every session to work in and through you. You are not guiding this group alone!

Group members will be spending one to three hours each unit studying *The Mind of Christ* with T. W. Hunt as their personal guide or tutor. The Holy Spirit will serve as their Teacher, for no spiritual truth can be understood without His involvement. The content and learning activities will help members learn the basic truths and principles during the week. Members will be working on application of the truths even before coming to the group time. Your job is to help members review what they have learned, share with each other what God is doing in their lives, and help each other make practical application of the truths to life.

You should expect that members will ask some questions you cannot answer. What you do in response will help them learn to turn to the Lord, His Word, and other believers for assistance. When you do not have an answer (or perhaps even when you do), encourage the group to join you in praying and searching the Scriptures together for an answer. A question may become an extra homework assignment for members to study during the week. Together, ask God to guide you to His answer, to His perspective. Then trust God to do it. When God sends the answer through one or more people in the group, you and your members will come to trust Him more.

### Grouping Members During the Session

In DURING THE SESSION, each activity has a recommended grouping. The size of the sub-groups is based on the content to be shared and the amount of time available. You may decide to use different groupings. If you do make a change, evaluate what members will be sharing, how much time you have, and what group size would provide for maximum member participation. The following descriptions explain the terms used in this guide.

- *Small Group*—Refers to a group of six to ten persons including the small-group leader. Unless a different group size is suggested, the activities during the session are for use with the entire small group.

- *Quads*—Refers to four people. Depending on the size of your group, each quad actually may have three, four, or five members. For instance, if you have eight members, you would have two quads of four each. For ten members we recommend two quads of three members and one quad with four. You could, however, have two groups of five. When you divide into quads, verbally give the assignment to all members. You may need to assign one member in each quad as the leader.

- *Pairs*—Refers to two people. If you have an odd number of people, one pair will need to have three members, or the extra person could work with you to form a pair.

Include yourself as you can in these small groupings for sharing and discussion. You will not only model a participating attitude, but you will also have the opportunity to share and grow with the group. They need to see you doing the same things you are asking them to do.

### Preparing for a Group Study of *The Mind of Christ*

As a small-group leader, you will need to prepare for the study, help enlist participants, guide the group sessions, and provide follow-up at the end of the study. The following suggestions should help you accomplish these tasks.

❧ **Prepare and secure resources.** Much of your course preparation can be completed at one time. First, complete the following actions:

❏ Prepare six session segment posters. Using poster board or newsprint prepare six posters—one for each of the first six segments of learning activities. Write a separate heading on each poster and copy the related Scripture passage. Display these posters on a focal wall for use during the Introductory Session. Then display them in your small-group room throughout the remainder of the study. The text for these posters is found on pages 12-13 LG.

❏ Prepare headings for the "Transformed To" wall and the "Transformed From" wall. On poster board or using construction paper letters, place titles on the left and right walls for the "Transforming by the Word" activity. See the description and diagram of the room set up that follows.

❑ Provide two tables in the room at which members can work.

❑ Provide two pieces of poster board or newsprint, masking tape, and markers for every session for the Transformed To and Transformed From lists.

❑ Prepare a poster listing the suggestions to help members memorize Scripture (see page 16 LG).

Read each BEFORE THE SESSION and prepare additional resources that are not listed here that you think you will need. If you add or adapt learning activities, you will need to prepare for those activities as well.

### ❧ Using the Learning Aids in This Guide

We have included several learning aids for you to use in a study of *The Mind of Christ*. Most of these are optional. Use them if you sense they will be helpful to your group.

• Reproduce the poster on page 4 LG for use in Session 11: Holiness and Love. You may want to display it on a focal wall throughout the study.

• Select the Masters for Additional Visual Support (pp. 48-59 LG) that you want to use in the Introductory Session. Prepare transparencies, handouts, or have them enlarged to poster size for use in a small group.

• Consider photocopying the Scriptures on pages 60-61 LG on a nice parchment-type paper for each member in your small group. If someone is willing and available, use watercolors or colored inks to enhance them. These can be framed and placed in church classrooms and at home as a visible reminder of Hebrews 10:24 and Philippians 2:5-11. You may want to present the first one (p. 60 LG) during the first session as you discuss the way your group will be applying that Scripture. The second one (p. 61 LG) can be used as a gift during Session 12 for members completing the study.

### ❧ Keep records. 
Work with the discipleship director or general secretary to determine the best way of keeping enrollment and attendance records. Participation in a LIFE course such as *The Mind of*

*Christ* counts toward Discipleship Training participation regardless of the time of week it is offered. Report your weekly attendance to the discipleship director or secretary.

Another reason to keep track of participation involves the Church Study Course system. Persons completing the individual study of *The Mind of Christ Member's Book* and attending the small-group sessions qualify for *The Mind of Christ Diploma*. These diplomas recognize members' significant work.

### ❧ Set up your room. 
Each week, set up your room similar to the diagram below:

Focal Wall: Six Segment Posters

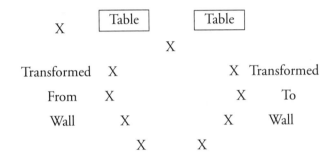

Place chairs (X) in a semi-circle with a focal wall at the open end. On the focal wall display the six posters that outline the segments of the small-group session. On the wall to the left place the title: *Transformed From*. On the wall to the right place the title: *Transformed To*. Add to these walls the lists that are prepared each week. Provide a table to the right and one to the left on which the quads can write their lists for Transforming by the Word. If possible, leave the lists in place throughout the study for the cumulative effect of reviewing what God is saying in His Word.

**Help Members Memorize Scripture**

One aspect of gaining the mind of Christ is implanting God's Word deeply in your mind. Some of your group may not be skilled at memorizing Scripture. Show them the cards in the back of the *Member's Book* and challenge members to memorize the key passages in *The Mind of Christ*. Review the ideas on page 10 of the *Member's Book* to help them further develop Scripture memorization. The ideas are listed in the next column for your convenience.

You might prepare a poster for your room containing these suggestions as a reminder of how to memorize Scripture. Review this poster several times during your study.

---

**How to Memorize Scripture**

1. Read the verse and think about the meaning.
2. Write the verse on notecards, one phrase per card.
3. Glance at the first phrase and say it aloud. Glance at the next phrase and say both phrases aloud. Continue this process until you have said the whole verse.
4. Try to say the verse from memory later in the day. If you cannot remember the complete verse, glance at the cards to refresh your memory.
5. Repeat the verse several times each day for a week or until you feel that the verse is firmly implanted in your mind.

---

**Clip Art**
You have permission to use the following clip art with your study of *The Mind of Christ.*

# THE MIND OF CHRIST

## THE MIND OF CHRIST

## THE MIND OF CHRIST

### THE MIND OF CHRIST

## STANDARD BEFORE AND AFTER THE SESSION

Cut on the dotted line and use these standard check-lists before and after each group session. You might want to laminate this cut-out section and use it as a bookmark for this guide.

## STANDARD BEFORE THE SESSION

The following suggestions for preparation are standard for each of the 12 small-group sessions. They will be referenced but not repeated.

❏ Complete the learning activities in the *Member's Book* and become familiar with any Lifelong Helps used during this unit.

❏ Pause and pray for God's guidance as you prepare for this week's group session. Pray specifically for each member of your group.

❏ Read DURING THE SESSION. You will have more suggestions than you will have time to complete. Select the activities and the order that best suits the learning and spiritual needs of your group. Adapt or develop other activities that will best help your group gain the greatest benefit from the unit. Decide on the amount of time to allow for each activity. Write a time in the margin to indicate when each activity should begin. (For example, write 6:20 beside "Stimulating to Love and Good Deeds.") Always be prepared to change your plans if the Holy Spirit should lead you in another direction.

❏ Arrange the room according to the chart on page 15 LG. Display the six session segment posters on the focal wall. Display as many lists from previous sessions as you can. These will serve as a reminder of the way God is working to conform members to the mind of Christ.

❏ Prepare a one-minute preview of the next unit.

## STANDARD AFTER THE SESSION

The following suggestions for evaluating a session are standard for each of the 12 small-group sessions. They will be referenced but not repeated.

❏ Record specific ways you can pray for each group member. Do you sense a need to pray for any one person in particular? If so, record these concerns.

❏ Ask yourself the following. Jot down your answers on a separate sheet of paper or in a journal.

• Do the activities need to be rearranged? Do some of them need more or less time?

• Did the groupings (quads, pairs, and small group) best meet the needs for participation, or would a different grouping have worked better?

• What spiritual or mental preparation do I need to make for the next session?

• Which of the members need to be encouraged to participate more in the sharing and discussion times? When and how will I encourage them?

• When could I have responded more appropriately to the needs of members or to the leadership of the Holy Spirit? What should I have done or said?

• How well did I do at beginning and ending on time?

• Would adjustments in our schedule, location, or room set up facilitate a better learning environment?

• Do I need to call or write one of the group members to offer encouragement, prayer, instruction, correction, or counsel? When shall I call? or write?

• Were there any absentees this week? Do I need to call with instructions or to check on possible needs?

• Did spiritual needs surface concerning our church as a body or its need for purification that I should share with church leadership for prayerful consideration?

❏ Read BEFORE THE SESSION for the next session to get an idea of advance preparation.

❏ Spend time alone with the Lord to seek His evaluation of your group leadership. Are you allowing God to guide you? Are you trusting God to work in members' lives? Do you need to make any adjustments to follow God's leadership better?

# INTRODUCTORY SESSION

# THE MIND OF CHRIST

## SESSION GOALS

This session will help potential members (1) understand the approach of the study and how it will help them more fully develop the mind of Christ; (2) understand the commitments required for participating in the LIFE course; and (3) demonstrate a commitment to complete the course requirements.

### BEFORE THE SESSION

❑ Prepare yourself spiritually for the upcoming study through a season of prayer. Ask God to draw people to the introductory session that He wants to involve in this study.

❑ Gather the following items:

• A copy of *The Mind of Christ Member's Book* for each potential small-group participant.

• The six session segment posters (p. 14 LG).

• The Scripture memory poster (see p. 16 LG).

• The Transform From and Transform To headings for the side walls (see p. 15 LG).

• Overhead transparencies, posters, or handouts to overview the course (pp. 48-59 LG).

• Create a poster or overhead transparency of the four images of how God might work to develop in believers the mind of Christ. (See 3 in During the Session).

❑ Set up your room according to the anticipated size of the group. This session includes all persons from your church interested in the study. Place the six session segment posters on a focal wall and the Transform From and Transform To headings on side walls.

❑ If you plan to use an overhead projector, secure a screen, projector, and extension cord.

❑ Prepare for the theme interpretation.

❑ Mark in your Bible the Scriptures you plan to read so you can turn to them quickly.

❑ Be prepared to register those who decide to participate in the course. Decide how you will collect book fees. Enlist a person to receive the fees after the session.

### DURING THE SESSION

**Arrival Activity (as members arrive plus 10 minutes)**

1. Greet prospective members as they arrive. Give a copy of *The Mind of Christ Member's Book* to every two people. Ask each pair to examine the contents pages and the various sections in the *Member's Book* that will help them in a lifelong process of developing the mind of Christ.

2. Opening Prayer. Pray that God will use this session to give insight into how members can develop the mind of Christ. Ask God to guide each person to respond to Him in making a decision about whether or not to study *The Mind of Christ* in the LIFE course format.

3. Theme Interpretation. Using a poster or overhead transparency of the four images that follow, describe in your own words how God might work in a person's life to develop the mind of Christ. If you choose, you could have some actors briefly act out these four images in visual vignettes.

• **Potter and the Clay.** Read Isaiah 64:8 and Jeremiah 18:6. Explain that just as a potter molds clay into a vessel of his choosing, God desires to mold us into the image of His Son Jesus Christ.

• **Husbandman and the Vine.** Read John 15:1-2. Explain that God acts as a husbandman (vine dresser or gardener) and we are the branches of the grapevine. God will prune (cut) away things (perhaps even good things) so that we may become more fruitful.

• **Washing of Water by the Word.** Read Ephesians 5:25-27. Explain that Christ uses God's Word to wash His people in order to cleanse them and sanctify them.

• **Sculptor and Marble.** Read 1 Corinthians 2:16. A famous sculptor was once asked how he could take a formless block of marble and sculpt a beautiful angel from it. The sculptor replied: "I see an angel inside the marble. I just cut away everything that isn't angel." God has placed His Son in us. We already have the mind of Christ.

**Course Overview (25 minutes)**

1. Overview the Content. Using the overhead transparencies, handouts, or posters you have prepared, briefly explain the following content elements:

• The outline of the hymn in Philippians 2:5-11 (Master 1, p. 49 LG). Explain that the hymn provides an outline for studying various aspects of the mind of Christ.

• Six Characteristics of the Christlike Mind (Master 2, p. 50 LG). Explain that these six words describe characteristics of the Christlike mind and that the course will help members develop these characteristics as they respond to God.

• Three Stages in Developing the Mind of Christ (Master 3, p. 51 LG). Explain that the course will guide members from the beginning stage toward the readiness stage as they develop maturity in Christ. Ask a member to read Colossians 3:2 as you describe "Beginning," another member to read Romans 12:2 as you describe "Growing," and a third member to read 1 Peter 1:13 as you describe "Qualified."

• Conforming to the Image of Christ (Master 4, p. 52 LG). Explain that this is a list of the ways members will seek to pattern their lives and minds after that of Christ's. Simply read the list.

• Unit Overviews (Master 5, p. 53 LG). Using the outline, provide a brief summary of the units in the *Member's Book.*

2. Course Requirements. Use the information under "The Lay Institute For Equipping" (p. 9 LG) to explain the requirements of self study and partici-

pation in the small-group sessions. Emphasize that participants will be expected to spend 30 to 60 minutes per day five days a week in completing assignments. Suggest that members who are not able to commit their time to the individual and small-group study should not participate at this time or should make the necessary adjustments so that they can complete the requirements. Offer to put names on a list for announcements of future studies when schedules may be more conducive to participation.

3. Time and Place. Announce when groups will be meeting to study *The Mind of Christ* using the LIFE course format. If you are offering other formats for the study, describe those and announce times and places. Explain how the LIFE-course approach offers a more personal, in-depth approach to developing the mind of Christ.

4. Questions. Call for and answer any questions people may have regarding the content of the course or the course requirements.

**Getting Ready for Next Week (20 minutes)**

Ask pairs to open the *Member's Books* to page 11. Using the following outline, describe the process for self-study that members will need to use during the coming week prior to the first small-group session.

**Unit Page.** Describe the various elements of the unit page. Guide members through the process of finding all the cards related to this first unit. Mention that the Scripture Memory cards for Philippians 2:5-11 are for use throughout the course. They do not have to memorize that passage all at once.

**Scripture Memory Verse.** Point out the Scripture memory verse on the unit page and on card 3A in the back of the book. Using the Scripture memory poster, suggest ways members can memorize Scripture.

**Daily Assignments.** Explain how content is divided into five daily assignments. Encourage members to study only one day at a time, so they will have time to think about and apply the teachings in their lives. Explain that if they decide to participate in the study their first assignment will be to complete the daily work for unit 1 before the first smal-group meeting.

**Learning Activities.** Point out one of the learning activities with the symbol (☙) and boldface type. Encourage members to complete all learning activities.

**Spiritual Journal.** Suggest that members may want to get a notebook or journal for recording responses to some of the assignments in the Lifelong Helps section.

**Prayer Partners.** Suggest that every group member should enlist a person to be a prayer partner with him or her during this study. This person could be a group member, spouse, or a close friend. Ask members to share regularly with this person specific ways they can pray for him or her as they work at developing the mind of Christ.

### Decision Time/Closing (5 minutes)

**Registration, Books, and Fees.** Describe the process for members to register for the course. Mention that those needing books should pick one up after the session. Announce the book fee and tell members how to pay the fee.

**Closing Prayer.** Call for a time of silent prayer. Ask those present to pray about their participation in the LIFE course study of *The Mind of Christ*. After a period of time, lead in a closing prayer requesting God's guidance during the coming weeks of study.

### AFTER THE SESSION

❏ Read and complete the evaluations and activities described in the Standard After the Session instructions (p. 18 LG).

❏ Save all posters for use in later sessions.

❏ Give the information from the registration sheets to the appropriate person in your church. If you have more than ten people per group, enlist additional leaders for every eight to ten people prior to the first small-group session.

❏ Secure additional resources as needed. If you do not have enough member's books, check with your local Baptist Book Store or Lifeway Christian Store for copies or call 1-800-458-2772 to place an order.

# BECOMING LIKE CHRIST

## SESSION GOALS

This session will help members understand how God will be working in their lives during this course to develop the mind of Christ. Members will demonstrate a willingness to help one another become like Christ.

### BEFORE THE SESSION

❏ Read and complete the activities in the Standard Before the Session instructions (p. 17 LG).

❏ Provide copies of *The Mind of Christ Member's Book* for any new members. Be prepared to give an orientation to the book and requirements for course participation.

❏ If you plan to give out copies of Hebrews 10:24, secure these before the session.

❏ Display the poster with instructions for Scripture memorization.

**Notes:** Remember, each time you divide the small group into pairs or quads, give verbal instructions to everyone. If you think they need the help, write the instructions on a chalkboard or newsprint. Unless otherwise indicated, the learning activities are recommended for the entire group.

### DURING THE SESSION

### Hearing What the Spirit Is Saying (as members arrive)

1. Register new members as they arrive. Distribute books to those who do not have them.

2. (Individuals) Ask members to review what God has been saying to them during the study of unit 1. Ask them to identify a Scripture and a name of Christ that have been meaningful this week. Then ask them to identify and mark the issue or subject in which God seems to be working most actively to develop the mind of Christ. These will be shared later in the session.

3. (Individuals) Ask members to write out any questions related to this unit they would like answered.

### Magnifying the Lord and Exalting His Name (5 minutes)

1. Read Psalm 34:3 from your session segment poster.

2. Open the session in prayer. Ask God to work in the minds and lives of members that they may reflect the mind of Christ. Acknowledge the presence of the Holy Spirit and ask Him to be your Teacher during the session. Encourage members to pray as they feel led to worship God for Who He is and acknowledge Him for what He has done. Encourage them to use the names of Christ to exalt His name together in prayer.

3. After prayer, invite members to share ways God revealed Himself this week through His names. Ask: Which name of Christ has been most meaningful to you and why?

### Transforming by the Word (15 minutes)

1. (Pairs) Ask members to pair up and quote this week's memory verse, Romans 12:2.

2. Ask members to share what God said to them through this week's memory verse or other Scripture that has been especially meaningful.

3. Using the poster you prepared, provide suggestions for memorizing Scripture (p. 16 LG).

3. Read Ephesians 5:25-27 from the session segment poster.

4. (Quads—two groups) Distribute poster board or newsprint and markers to each of two quads. Ask members to help you make two lists related to

characteristics of a Christlike mind. Focus on this unit's Scriptures only. Ask one quad to make a list of things, actions, or attitudes identified or implied in Scriptures during unit 1 that need to be *cleansed from* one's mind and life. Ask the second quad to make a list of things, actions, or attitudes identified or implied in Scriptures in unit 1 that need to be *incorporated into* one's mind and life. For example: We need to transform ourselves from being carnally minded to being spiritually minded (see Rom. 8:6).

5. Call on quads to read and comment on their lists. Place one on the Transformed From Wall and the other on the Transformed To Wall.

6. Ask a volunteer to pray that God will cleanse members of your group and church.

## Stimulating One Another to Love and Good Deeds (20 minutes)

1. Read Hebrews 10:24 from your session segment poster. Explain that God puts members together in the body of Christ so they can help each other become all that God wants them to be. Members of the body of Christ need each other. During this course, members will have opportunity to help each other in the lifelong process of developing the mind of Christ. Emphasize the fact that this will include both giving help to and receiving help from a brother or sister in Christ. If you made plans to hand out copies of Hebrews 10:24, distribute those to members.

2. Read Ephesians 5:8-21 and point out the importance of believers being submissive to one another in the fear of God.

3. Pause and pray that God will help group members learn to function as the body should in both giving and receiving help from one another. Pray that God will develop in your group a spirit of lowliness before God and humility before one another with mutual submission to one another.

4. State that this course is only an introduction to a lifelong process of developing the mind of Christ. Encourage members to focus on the long-term growth God is seeking.

5. Invite volunteers to share testimonies of what God has done this week in their lives that has been meaningful, challenging, or instructive.

6. Encourage members to state questions or concerns they have written for consideration. As time permits, guide the group in answering the questions.

7. As time permits, discuss one or more of the following questions:

• Why do you want to develop the mind of Christ? or Why have you decided to participate in this course?

• Which of the six characteristics of the Christlike mind seems to be the most rare in the church today? Why do you think that is true? What do you think could be done better to develop that characteristic in believers' lives?

• Which of the three principles (Will, River, or Readiness, pp. 22-24) is most needed in your life right now and why? What are some ways we can: (1) set our minds on things above? (2) experience the renewing of our minds? (3) gird up our minds for action?

• What role do you have in developing the mind of Christ? What is God's role? (See p. 26)

8. Ask members to turn in their *Member's Books* to page 26 and share their response to the first activity.

## Preparing the Bride for Her Bridegroom (5 minutes)

1. Call on a person to read Revelation 19:1-9. Ask members to listen for ways the bride (church) needs to prepare for the return of Christ.

2. Share in your own words the parable of the bride found in the next to the last paragraph in "From the Writer" (p. 5 LG). Emphasize the role this course can play in helping the Bride get ready.

3. As time permits, ask and discuss these questions:

• What needs to be done between now and the marriage supper of the Lamb in order for the bride to be ready?

• What cleansing, purifying, or preparation is needed in our church?

• How can we apply this Scripture to our lives, families, and church?

4. Call on one member to pray for your church to continue to prepare for the Lord's return.

**Praying for One Another (10 minutes)**

1. (Quads) Ask members to share personal, family, church, or work-related prayer requests that primarily focus on developing the mind of Christ or purifying the bride. Read James 5:16 and suggest that members may want to confess their need to become more like Christ in specific ways.

2. (Quads) Ask quads to pray specifically for one another for forgiveness, healing, encouragement, guidance, wisdom, knowledge, understanding, courage, strength, faithfulness, or for specific requests.

**Closing the Session (5 minutes)**

1. Invite members to share questions or concerns discussed during the session that the group should remember in prayer.

2. Preview unit 2 in the *Member's Book*. Point out the Lifelong Helps (Bondage to Freedom Lists) on pages 186-188 that will be used for the first time during unit 2.

3. Close by praying that God will work throughout this study to set, renew, and gird up the minds of group members to grow more like Christ.

❏ Read and complete the evaluations and activities described in the Standard After the Session instructions (p. 18 LG).

❏ Does everyone in your group have a *Member's Book?* If not, secure needed books and, if possible, deliver them to the members early in the week.

❏ Do you need to secure other resources for the group sessions this week?

# FREEDOM IN CHRIST

## SESSION GOALS

This session will help members understand how their conflicting desires can produce a disordered mind and how Christ can set them free from bondage to sin. Members will demonstrate a willingness to seek first the Kingdom.

**BEFORE THE SESSION**

❏ Read and complete the activities in the Standard Before the Session instructions (p. 17 LG).

❏ Make sure each member has a copy of *The Mind of Christ Member's Book*. New members need to understand the importance of completing the learning activities in the unit prior to the group session.

**Note:** After this session no new members should be accepted, since they will have too much work to do to catch up with the rest of the group. Be prepared to take names of interested persons for the next time the course is offered.

**DURING THE SESSION**

**Hearing What the Spirit Is Saying (as members arrive)**

1. (Individuals) Ask members to review what God has been saying to them during the study of unit 2. Ask them to identify a Scripture and a name of Christ that have been most meaningful this week. Then ask them to identify and mark the issue or subject in which God seems to be working most actively to develop the mind of Christ. These will be shared later in the session.

2. (Individuals) Ask members to write out any questions for which they would like to find answers.

**Magnifying the Lord and Exalting His Name (5 minutes)**

1. Open the session by asking God to use this study to set members free from bondage to sin, especially the lusts and desires that are contrary to the mind of Christ. Encourage members to pray as they feel led to worship God for who He is and acknowledge Him for what He has done. Encourage them to use the names of Christ to exalt His name together in prayer.

2. After prayer, invite members to share ways God revealed Himself this week through His names. Ask: Which name of Christ has been most meaningful to you and why?

**Transforming by the Word (15 minutes)**

1. (Pairs) Ask members to pair up and quote this week's memory verse, Matthew 6:33.

2. Ask members to review last week's memory verse by quoting Romans 12:2 in unison.

3. Ask members to share what God said to them through this week's memory verse or other Scripture that has been meaningful.

4. Read Ephesians 5:26 from the session segment poster.

5. (Quads—two groups) Distribute poster board or newsprint and markers to each of two quads. Ask members to help you make two lists related to the disordered mind of humanity and the ordered mind of Christ. Focus on this unit's Scriptures only. Ask one quad to make a list of things, actions, or attitudes identified or implied in Scriptures during unit 2 that need to be *cleansed from* one's mind and life. Ask the second quad to make a list of things, actions, or attitudes identified or implied in Scriptures in unit 2 that need to be *incorporated into* one's mind and life. For example: We need to abandon living after the flesh and embrace living after the spirit (see Rom. 8:1).

6. Call on quads to read and comment on their lists. Place one on the Transformed From Wall and the other on the Transformed To Wall.

7. Ask a volunteer to pray that God will cleanse members of your group and church.

**Stimulating One Another to Love and Good Deeds (20 minutes)**

1. Read Hebrews 10:24.

2. Invite volunteers to share testimonies of what God has done this week in their lives that has been meaningful, challenging, or instructive.

3. Encourage members to state questions or concerns they have written for consideration. As time permits, guide the group in answering the questions.

4. As time permits, discuss one or more of the following questions:

- What are some examples of conflicting desires that you found as you developed your desires lists? Do these conflicting desires cause mental conflict?

- What are some overall observations you made about your desires after you completed your list? Were your desires primarily God-honoring or self-serving?

- How can the "Process Toward Freedom" (p. 34) help you let Christ set you free? How did you respond to the third activity on page 36?

- What is the value of asking Christ to "fix your wanter"?

- What, if anything, has God impressed you to do to begin seeking His kingdom first?

**Preparing the Bride for Her Bridegroom (5 minutes)**

1. Call on a person to read Matthew 25:1-13. Ask members to listen for ways the bride (church) needs to prepare for the return of Christ.

2. As time permits, ask and discuss these questions:

- Though the bridegroom may tarry, how important is it for us to be ready?

- What cleansing, purifying, or preparation is needed in our church?

- How can we apply this Scripture to our lives, families, and church?

3. Call on one member to pray for your church to continue to prepare for the Lord's return.

**Praying for One Another (10 minutes)**

1. (Quads) Ask members to share personal, family, church, or work-related prayer requests that primarily focus on developing the mind of Christ or purifying the bride. Read James 5:16 and suggest that members may want to confess struggles they are having between the flesh and the spirit.

2. (Quads) Ask quads to pray specifically for one another for forgiveness, healing, encouragement, guidance, wisdom, knowledge, understanding, courage, strength, faithfulness, or for specific requests.

**Closing the Session (5 minutes)**

1. Invite members to share questions or concerns that came up during the session that the group should remember in prayer.

2. Preview unit 3. Suggest to members that they may want to keep the lists they will be making in a journal or loose leaf binder so they can review and update them periodically.

3. Close by praying Matthew 6:33. Ask God to enable every member to seek His kingdom first.

**AFTER THE SESSION**

❏ Read and complete the evaluations and activities described in the Standard After the Session instructions (p. 18 LG).

❏ If you have others who want to begin the study, give their names to the discipleship director for enlistment in the next class. Explain that the homework requirements would be too heavy to catch up at this time. You may want to recommend that they use the conference videos or audiocassettes.

❏ Are members having difficulty memorizing Scripture? If so, schedule time in the next session to review your poster with instructions for Scripture memorization. You may want to ask members to share their successes for Scripture memory with one another.

# FREE INDEED

## SESSION GOALS

This session will help members understand areas of bondage to sin and how Christ wants to work to set them free. Members will demonstrate submission to God's working in their lives.

**BEFORE THE SESSION**

❑ Read and complete the activities in the Standard Before the Session instructions (p. 17 LG).

**DURING THE SESSION**

**Hearing What the Spirit Is Saying (as members arrive)**

1. (Individuals) Ask members to review what God has been saying to them during the study of unit 3. Ask them to identify a Scripture and a name of Christ that have been most meaningful this week. Then ask them to identify and mark the issue or subject in which God seems to be working most actively to develop the mind of Christ. These will be shared later in the session.

2. (Individuals) Ask members to write out any questions for which they would like to find answers.

**Magnifying the Lord and Exalting His Name (5 minutes)**

1. Open the session by asking God to continue the process of setting members free from bondage to sin in every area of life. Encourage members to pray prayers of praise and thanksgiving to God. Encourage them to use the names of Christ to exalt His name together in prayer.

2. After prayer, invite members to share ways God revealed Himself this week through His names. Ask: Which name of Christ has been most meaningful to you and why?

**Transforming by the Word (15 minutes)**

1. (Pairs) Ask members to pair up and quote this week's memory verse, John 8:32,36. As time permits, ask them to alternate quoting verses from previous units. Encourage them to use their Scripture memory cards as a reference.

2. Ask members to share what God said to them through this week's memory verse or other Scripture that has been meaningful.

3. (Quads—two groups) Distribute poster board or newsprint and markers to each of two quads. Ask members to help you make two lists related to areas of sin's bondage. Focus on this unit's Scriptures only. Ask one quad to make a list of things, actions, or attitudes identified or implied in Scriptures during unit 3 that need to be *cleansed from* one's mind and life. Ask the second quad to make a list of things, actions, or attitudes identified or implied in Scriptures in unit 3 that need to be *incorporated into* one's mind and life. For example: We need to cleanse ourselves from our love for the world and the things of the world and incorporate love for God (see 1 John).

4. Call on quads to read and comment on their lists. Place one on the Transformed From Wall and the other on the Transformed To Wall.

5. Ask a volunteer to pray that God will cleanse members of your group and church.

**Stimulating One Another to Love and Good Deeds (20 minutes)**

1. Read Hebrews 10:24.

2. Invite volunteers to share testimonies of what God has done this week in their lives that has been meaningful, challenging, or instructive.

3. Encourage members to state questions or concerns they have written for consideration. As time permits, guide the group in answering the questions.

4. As time permits discuss one or more of the following questions:

• Why should we not rush God in the process of receiving freedom from bondage to sin? (pp. 47-48)

• How could giving up your responsibilities hinder or thwart what God wants to do in developing in you the mind of Christ? (p. 47)

• What experiences have been meaningful this week as you have prepared your lists? What has God been doing in your life to set you free?

5. Ask members to turn to page 56 and share their responses to the second activity.

6. Remind members that they are only receiving an introduction to a lifelong process. They should not expect a quick fix or instant success in all areas. Remind them to let God work on His schedule as they are responsive to Him.

7. Ask members to share the one area where they face their greatest challenge for being freed from bondage to sin. They do not have to be specific. If you sense it is appropriate, take time to pray for each other.

**Preparing the Bride for Her Bridegroom (5 minutes)**

1. Call on a person to read 2 Peter 3:1-14. Ask members to listen for ways the bride (church) needs to prepare for the return of Christ.

2. As time permits, ask and discuss these questions:

• Seeing that the world will come to an end, what kind of persons ought we be?

• What cleansing, purifying, or preparation is needed in our church?

• How can we apply this Scripture to our lives, families, and church?

3. Call on one member to pray for your church to continue to prepare for the Lord's return.

**Praying for One Another (10 minutes)**

1. (Quads) Ask members to share personal, family, church, or work-related prayer requests that primarily focus on developing the mind of Christ or purifying the bride. Read James 5:16 and suggest that members may want to confess faults, weaknesses, sins, struggles, and failures.

2. (Quads) Ask quads to pray specifically for one another for forgiveness, healing, encouragement, guidance, wisdom, knowledge, understanding, courage, strength, faithfulness, or for specific requests.

**Closing the Session (5 minutes)**

1. Invite members to share questions or concerns that came up during the session that the group should remember in prayer.

2. Preview unit 4.

3. Close by praying that God will work this week to develop in each member the virtues of godly wisdom.


**AFTER THE SESSION**

❏ Read and complete the evaluations and activities described in the Standard After the Session instructions (p. 18 LG).

❏ Did any difficulty or serious need arise during the sharing this week related to one of the areas like fears, hurts, or weaknesses? Do you need to follow up with a call or a visit? How can you pray for the need?

# VIRTUES OF GODLY WISDOM

## SESSION GOALS

This session will help members understand the difference between the virtues of godly wisdom in James 3:17 and their opposites and perversions. Members will demonstrate a spiritual hunger for Christ to establish these virtues in their minds and lives.

### BEFORE THE SESSION

❏ Read and complete the activities in the Standard Before the Session instructions (p. 17 LG).

### DURING THE SESSION

### Hearing What the Spirit Is Saying (as members arrive)

1. (Individuals) Ask members to review what God has been saying to them during the study of unit 4. Ask them to identify a Scripture and a name of Christ that have been most meaningful this week. Then ask them to identify and mark the virtue, issue, or subject in which God seems to be working most actively to develop the mind of Christ. These will be shared later in the session.

2. (Individuals) Ask members to write out any questions for which they would like to find answers.

### Magnifying the Lord and Exalting His Name (5 minutes)

1. Open the session by asking God to work through each member to develop the virtues of godly wisdom. Encourage members to pray as they feel led to worship God for who He is and acknowledge Him for what He has done. Encourage them to use the names of Christ to exalt His name together in prayer.

2. After prayer, invite members to share ways God revealed Himself this week through His names. Ask: Which name of Christ has been most meaningful to you and why?

### Transforming by the Word (15 minutes)

1. (Pairs) Ask members to pair up and quote this week's memory verse, James 3:17. Then, as time permits, ask them to alternate quoting verses from previous units. Encourage them to use their Scripture memory cards as a reference.

2. Ask members to share what God said to them through this week's memory verse or other Scripture that has been meaningful.

3. (Quads—two groups) Distribute a poster board or newsprint and markers to each of two quads. Ask members to help you make two lists related to virtues, their satanic opposites, and their perversions. Focus on this unit's Scriptures only but include those in the Lifelong Helps for this unit. Ask one quad to make a list of things, actions, or attitudes identified or implied in Scriptures during unit 4 that need to be *cleansed from* one's mind and life. Ask the second quad to make a list of things, actions, or attitudes identified or implied in Scriptures in unit 4 that need to be *incorporated into* one's mind and life. For example: We need to abandon youthful lusts and embrace righteousness, faith, charity, and peace (see 2 Tim. 2:22).

4. Call on quads to read and comment on their lists. Place one list on the Transformed From Wall and the other on the Transformed To Wall.

5. Ask a volunteer to pray that God will cleanse members of your group and church.

**Stimulating One Another to Love and Good Deeds (20 minutes)**

1. Ask the group to quote Hebrews 10:24.

2. Invite volunteers to share testimonies of what God has done this week in their lives that has been meaningful, challenging, or instructive.

3. Encourage members to state questions or concerns they have written for consideration. As time permits, guide the group in answering the questions.

4. As time permits discuss one or more of the following questions:

• What is a good reason for becoming familiar with what God has said in the Bible? (p. 63)

• How has humanism affected your thinking and living? What can we do to let God renew our thinking?

• Which of the virtues does God seem to be working on in your life right now?

• With all the impurity surrounding us, what can we do as Christians to develop and maintain purity?

• Which of the perversions do you see most frequently in the Christian community? Why do you think that is true?

• If God were to measure our church by the standards of these virtues, what do you think He would have to say to us as a church? What can we do to help each other? to help our families?

5. Ask members to turn to page 65 and share how they responded to the first activity.

**Preparing the Bride for Her Bridegroom (5 minutes)**

1. Call on a person to read 1 Thessalonians 4:1–5:11. Ask members to listen for ways the bride (church) needs to prepare for the return of Christ.

2. As time permits, ask and discuss these questions:

• With what words should we comfort each other regarding the second coming?

• What cleansing, purifying, or preparation is needed in our church?

• How can we apply this Scripture to our lives, families, and church?

3. Call on one member to pray for your church to continue to prepare for the Lord's return.

**Praying for One Another (10 minutes)**

1. Read James 5:16 from your session segment poster.

2. (Quads) Ask members to share personal, family, church, or work related prayer requests that primarily focus on developing the mind of Christ or purifying the bride.

3. (Quads) Ask quads to pray specifically for one another for forgiveness, healing, encouragement, guidance, wisdom, knowledge, understanding, courage, strength, faithfulness, or for specific requests.

**Closing the Session (5 minutes)**

1. Invite members to share questions or concerns that came up during the session that the group should remember in prayer.

2. Preview unit 5. Remind members that God's agenda is far more important than just following a course outline. Suggest that they study unit 5, but spend time working on any area in which God seems to be focusing their attention. For instance, God may want a person to continue working on purity. Give permission for members to spend time on God's agenda, even if they are distracted from the current unit of study.

3. Close by praying that God will manifest His Spirit and reveal His fruit in the lives of members this next week.

**AFTER THE SESSION**

❏ Read and complete the evaluations and activities described in the Standard After the Session instructions (p. 18 LG).

# GROUP SESSION 5

# FRUIT OF THE SPIRIT

## SESSION GOALS

This session will help members understand the difference between the virtues in Galatians 5:22-23 and their opposites and perversions. Members will demonstrate a spiritual hunger for Christ to establish and manifest these virtues in their minds and their lives.

BEFORE THE SESSION

❑ Read and complete the activities in the Standard Before the Session instructions (p. 17 LG).

DURING THE SESSION

Hearing What the Spirit Is Saying (as members arrive)

1. (Individuals) Ask members to review what God has been saying to them during the study of unit 5. Ask them to identify a Scripture and a name of Christ that has been meaningful this week. Then ask them to identify and mark the fruit, virtue, issue, or subject in which God seems to be working most actively to develop the mind of Christ. These will be shared later in the session.

Magnifying the Lord and Exalting His Name (5 minutes)

1. Open the session in prayer asking God to so cleanse lives that His Spirit will be seen clearly in every life as He manifests His fruit. Encourage members to pray as they feel led to thank God for what He has been doing to reveal Himself and His ways to them during this study. Encourage them to use the names of Christ to exalt His name together in prayer.

2. After prayer, invite members to share ways God may have revealed Himself this week through His names. Ask: Which name of Christ has been most meaningful to you and why?

Transforming by the Word (15 minutes)

1. (Pairs) Ask members to pair up and quote this week's memory verse, Galatians 5:22-23.

2. Ask volunteers to quote each of the verses from previous units: Romans 12:2; Matthew 6:33; John 8:32,36; and James 3:17.

3. Ask members to share what God said to them through this week's memory verse or other Scripture that has been meaningful.

4. (Quads—two groups) Distribute poster board or newsprint and markers to each of two quads. Make sure members have a chance to work on different lists occasionally rather than always working on Transformed From or Transformed To. Ask members to help you make two lists related to the fruit of the Spirit, their satanic opposites, and their perversions. Focus on this unit's Scriptures only. Ask one quad to make a list of things, actions, or attitudes identified or implied in Scriptures during unit 5 that need to be *cleansed from* one's mind and life. Ask the second quad to make a list of things, actions, or attitudes identified or implied in Scriptures in unit 5 that need to be *incorporated into* one's mind and life. For example: We need to eliminate hate for our enemies and cultivate love for our enemies (see Matt. 5:43-44).

4. Call on quads to read and comment on their lists. Place one on the Transformed From Wall and the other on the Transformed To Wall.

5. Ask a volunteer to pray that God will cleanse members of your group and church.

**Stimulating One Another to Love and Good Deeds (20 minutes)**

1. Ask someone to quote Hebrews 10:24.

2. Invite volunteers to share testimonies of what God has done this week in their lives that has been meaningful, challenging, or instructive.

3. Encourage members to state questions or concerns that they have written for consideration. As time permits, guide the group in answering the questions.

4. As time permits, discuss one or more of the following questions:

• What are some of the things God has been doing in your life this week to develop any of the 17 Christ-like virtues?

• Which of the virtues does God seem to be working on in your life right now?

• Which of the virtues is most lacking in our church today? Which is most visible?

• Which of the perversions do you see most frequently in the Christian community? Why do you think that is true?

• If God were to measure our church by the standards of these virtues, what do you think He would He have to say to us as a church? What can we do to help each other? to help our families?

• How clearly do we allow the Spirit to manifest these fruits through us? If we don't measure up very well, what do you sense God would have us do as a church? as individuals? as families?

**Preparing the Bride for Her Bridegroom (5 minutes)**

1. Call on a person to read 2 Timothy 3:1-17. Ask members to listen for ways the bride (church) needs to prepare for the return of Christ.

2. As time permits, ask and discuss these questions:

• What are the marks of the last days and what can the church do to prepare for that time?

• Do you see any evidences that could indicate we may be living in the last days? What?

• What cleansing, purifying, or preparation is needed in our church?

• How can we apply this Scripture to our lives, families, and church?

3. Call on one member to pray for your church to continue to prepare for the Lord's return.

**Praying for One Another (10 minutes)**

1. (Quads) Ask members to share personal, family, church, or work-related prayer requests that primarily focus on developing the mind of Christ or purifying the bride.

2. (Quads) Ask quads to pray specifically for one another for forgiveness, healing, encouragement, guidance, wisdom, knowledge, understanding, courage, strength, faithfulness, or for specific requests.

**Closing the Session (5 minutes)**

1. Invite members to share questions or concerns that came up during the session that the group should remember in prayer.

2. Preview unit 6. Encourage members to watch for ways this week to demonstrate a spirit of servanthood.

3. Close by praying that God will help members follow the model of Jesus in being servants.

**AFTER THE SESSION**

❏ Read and complete the evaluations and activities described in the Standard After the Session instructions (p. 18 LG).

❏ Consider having a social get-together for your group about half way through the study (session 6 or 7). Involve group members in planning for the time together.

32

# THE SERVANT MIND

## SESSION GOALS

This session will help members understand the characteristics of the servant mind. Members will demonstrate submission to God as their Master and Lord.

**BEFORE THE SESSION**

❏ Read and complete the activities in the Standard Before the Session instructions (p. 17 LG).

❏ Prepare to discuss a possible get-together for your group or to share plans for such an event.

❏ Provide notebook paper and a pencil for each member to use in completing the Servanthood Instrument.

**DURING THE SESSION**

**Hearing What the Spirit Is Saying (as members arrive)**

1. (Individuals) Ask members to turn to the Servanthood Instrument in the Lifelong Helps section of the *Member's Book* (p. 201). Ask them to read the instructions and complete the test as a personal evaluation of their attitudes about servanthood. Provide notebook paper so members can keep a clean copy of the test in their books for future use.

2. (Individuals) If members finish the test before the beginning of the session, ask them to review what God has been saying to them during the study of unit 6. Ask them to identify a Scripture and a name of Christ that have been meaningful this week. Then ask them to identify and mark the servant attitude, issue, or subject in which God seems to be working most actively to develop the mind of Christ. These will be shared later in the session.

3. (Individuals) Ask members to write out any questions for which they would like to find answers.

**Magnifying the Lord and Exalting His Name (5 minutes)**

1. Open the session by asking God to develop the attitude of servanthood in every member. Encourage members to pray as they feel led to worship God for who He is and acknowledge Him for what He has done. Encourage them to use the names of Christ to exalt His name together in prayer.

2. After prayer, invite members to share ways God revealed Himself this week through His names. Ask: Which name of Christ has been most meaningful to you and why?

**Transforming by the Word (15 minutes)**

1. (Pairs) Ask members to pair up and quote this week's memory verse, Matthew 10:25. Then, as time permits, ask them to alternate quoting verses from previous units. Encourage them to use their Scripture memory cards as a reference.

2. Ask members to share what God said to them through this week's memory verse or other Scripture that has been meaningful.

3. (Quads—two groups) Distribute poster board or newsprint and markers to each of two quads. Ask members to help you make two lists related to servanthood. Focus on this unit's Scriptures only. Ask one quad to make a list of things, actions, or attitudes identified or implied in Scriptures during unit 6 that need to be *cleansed from* one's mind and life. Ask the second quad to make a list of things, actions, or attitudes identified or implied in Scriptures in unit 6 that need to be *incorporated into* one's mind and life.

For example: We need to stop ruling by exercising authority and start serving humbly (see Matt. 20:25-28).

4. Call on quads to read and comment on their lists. Place one on the Transformed From Wall and the other on the Transformed To Wall.

5. Ask a volunteer to pray that God will cleanse members of your group and church.

## Stimulating One Another to Love and Good Deeds (20 minutes)

1. Read Hebrews 10:24.

2. Invite volunteers to share testimonies of what God has done this week in their lives that has been meaningful, challenging, or instructive.

3. Encourage members to state questions or concerns they have written for consideration. As time permits, guide the group in answering the questions.

4. As time permits discuss one or more of the following questions:

• What are some of the clearest ways Jesus demonstrated the servant mind by His actions?

• Why should Christians want to become servants?

• Why has the art of being a servant disappeared from our society?

• How do most people outside the church seek greatness? How do most people inside the church seek greatness? Do Christians live more by God's ways or the world's ways?

• Would people in our community see our church as one that serves people? Why or why not? Is there anything we need to do to change that perception?

• Which of the characteristics of the servant mind is God working on in your life?

5. Ask members to think about each of the characteristics, one at a time. Ask: How can we help each other develop these characteristics? What is God's role, and what is our role?

## Preparing the Bride for Her Bridegroom (5 minutes)

1. Call on a person to read Matthew 25:31-46. Ask members to listen for ways the bride (church) needs to minister to others as they await the return of Christ.

2. As time permits, ask and discuss these questions:

• What kinds of service characterize true believers who willingly serve the Lord?

• What areas of service are we neglecting that as a church Christ is expecting?

• What cleansing, purifying, or preparation is needed in our church?

• How can we apply this Scripture to our lives, families, and church?

3. Call on one member to pray for your church to minister in the name and character of Christ to those who have needs.

## Praying for One Another (10 minutes)

1. (Quads) Read James 5:16 from your session segment poster and ask members to share personal, family, church, or work-related prayer requests that primarily focus on developing the mind of Christ or purifying the bride.

2. (Quads) Ask quads to pray specifically for one another regarding the specific requests made and for the development of a servant spirit in every member.

## Closing the Session (5 minutes)

1. Invite members to share questions or concerns that came up during the session that the group should remember in prayer.

2. Preview unit 7 by using the overview of the Beatitudes in the Lifelong Helps section (pp. 202-212).

3. Mention the get-together. Enlist help in planning and preparing for the event if you choose to do it.

4. Close by praying that God will use circumstances to develop the character of Christ and the attitudes described in the Beatitudes in your group members.

### AFTER THE SESSION

❑ Read and complete the evaluations and activities described in the Standard After the Session instructions (p. 18 LG).

❑ Finalize plans for the get-together.

# GROUP SESSION 7
# THE BEATITUDES

## SESSION GOALS

This session will help members understand ways God uses circumstances to develop the Beatitudes in their lives. Members will demonstrate an openness to God's work of developing the Beatitudes in their lives.

**BEFORE THE SESSION**

❏ Read and complete the activities in the Standard Before the Session instructions (p. 17 LG).

❏ Consider making enlarged posters of the contrasts between the first four and the second four Beatitudes. Use the transparency masters on pages 57-58 LG as a guide.

**DURING THE SESSION**
## Hearing What the Spirit Is Saying (as members arrive)

1. (Individuals) Ask members to review what God has been saying to them during the study of unit 7. Ask them to identify a Scripture and a name of Christ that have been meaningful this week. Then ask them to identify and mark the Beatitude, virtue, issue, or subject in which God seems to be working most actively to develop the mind of Christ. These will be shared later in the session.

2. (Individuals) Ask members to write out any questions for which they would like to find answers.

## Magnifying the Lord and Exalting His Name (5 minutes)

1. Open the session by asking God to reveal to members how He works through circumstances to develop the Beatitudes in believers. Encourage members to pray as they feel led to worship God for who He is and acknowledge Him for what He has done. Encourage them to use the names of Christ to exalt His name together in prayer.

2. After prayer, invite members to share ways God revealed Himself this week through His names. Ask: Which name of Christ has been most meaningful to you and why?

## Transforming by the Word (15 minutes)

1. (Pairs) Ask members to pair up and quote this week's memory verse, Matthew 5:3. Then, as time permits, ask them to alternate quoting verses from previous units. Encourage them to use their Scripture memory cards as a reference.

2. Ask members to share what God said to them through this week's memory verse or other Scripture that has been meaningful.

3. (Quads—two groups) Distribute poster board or newsprint and markers to each of two quads. Ask members to help you make two lists related to the Beatitudes. Focus on this unit's Scriptures only. Ask one quad to make a list of things, actions, or attitudes identified or implied in Scriptures during unit 7 that need to be *cleansed from* one's mind and life. Ask the second quad to make a list of things, actions, or attitudes identified or implied in Scriptures in unit 7 that need to be *incorporated into* one's mind and life. For example: We need to stop exalting self and start humbling self (see Luke 18:10-14).

4. Call on quads to read and comment on their lists. Place one on the Transformed To Wall and the other on the Transformed From Wall.

5. Ask a volunteer to pray that God will cleanse members of your group and church.

**Stimulating One Another to Love and Good Deeds (20 minutes)**

1. Ask the group to quote Hebrews 10:24.

2. Invite volunteers to share testimonies of what God has done this week in their lives that has been meaningful, challenging, or instructive.

3. Encourage members to state questions or concerns they have written for consideration. As time permits, guide the group in answering the questions.

4. Using the two posters contrasting the first four and the second four Beatitudes, guide the group in discussing the helpfulness of these divisions. Use the material on page 112 as a guide for your questions and discussion.

5. Ask members to turn to page 115. Ask volunteers to share their responses to the first activity.

6. As time permits, discuss one or more of the following questions:

• How does God use circumstances to develop the Beatitudes in a person's life? Give an example.

• In the second four Beatitudes, why is it important for a person to identify with Christ by expressing the Beatitude? Give an example.

• Why do you think God repeatedly guides us through the cycle of developing the Beatitudes?

• What can we do to help one another respond to God's activity in developing the Beatitudes?

• Which of the Beatitudes is God working on in your life right now? Would some of you share how He seems to be working in or through you?

**Preparing the Bride for Her Bridegroom (5 minutes)**

1. Call on a person to read Matthew 24:1-35. Ask members to listen for ways the bride (church) needs to prepare for the return of Christ.

2. As time permits, ask and discuss these questions:

• What evidences do you observe that may indicate Christ's return may be drawing near?

• What cleansing, purifying, or preparation is needed in our church?

• How can we apply this Scripture to our lives, families, and church?

3. Call on one member to pray for your church to continue to prepare for the Lord's return.

**Praying for One Another (10 minutes)**

1. (Quads) Read James 5:16 from your session segment poster and ask members to share personal, family, church, or work-related prayer requests that primarily focus on developing the mind of Christ or purifying the bride.

2. (Quads) Ask quads to pray specifically for one another for forgiveness, healing, encouragement, guidance, wisdom, knowledge, understanding, courage, strength, faithfulness, or for specific requests.

**Closing the Session (5 minutes)**

1. Invite members to share questions or concerns that came up during the session that the group should remember in prayer.

2. Preview unit 8. Encourage members to watch for ways they exhibit both positive and negative emotions this week.

3. Close by praying that this week God will help members learn to control emotional impulses that do not reflect the mind or character of Christ.

**AFTER THE SESSION**

❏ Read and complete the evaluations and activities described in the Standard After the Session instructions (p. 18 LG).

# GROUP SESSION 8
# JESUS AND EMOTIONS

## SESSION GOALS

This session will help members understand ways to control emotional impulses and properly express both negative and positive emotions. Members will demonstrate a desire to control all emotional expressions properly.

### BEFORE THE SESSION
❑ Read and complete the activities in the Standard Before the Session instructions (p. 17 LG).

### DURING THE SESSION
#### Hearing What the Spirit Is Saying (as members arrive)

1. (Individuals) Ask members to review what God has been saying to them during the study of unit 8. Ask them to identify a Scripture and a name of Christ that have been meaningful this week. Then ask them to identify and mark the emotion, issue, or subject in which God seems to be working most actively to develop the mind of Christ. These will be shared later in the session.

2. (Individuals) Ask members to write out any questions for which they would like to find answers.

#### Magnifying the Lord and Exalting His Name (5 minutes)

1. Open the session by asking God to teach members how to reflect Christ in the way they express emotions. Encourage members to pray as they feel led to worship God for who He is and acknowledge Him for what He has done. Encourage them to use the names of Christ to exalt His name together in prayer.

2. After prayer, invite members to share ways God revealed Himself this week through His names. Ask: Which name of Christ has been most meaningful and why?

#### Transforming by the Word (15 minutes)

1. (Pairs) Ask members to pair up and quote this week's memory verse, John 1:14. Then, as time permits, ask them to alternate quoting verses from previous units. Encourage them to use their Scripture memory cards as a reference.

2. Ask members to share what God said to them through this week's memory verse or other Scripture that has been meaningful.

3. (Quads—two groups) Distribute poster board or newsprint and markers to each of two quads. Ask members to help you make two lists related to expression of emotions. Focus on this unit's Scriptures only. Ask one quad to make a list of things, actions, or attitudes identified or implied in Scriptures during unit 8 that need to be *cleansed from* one's mind and life. Ask the second quad to make a list of things, actions, or attitudes identified or implied in Scriptures in unit 8 that need to be *incorporated into* one's mind and life. For example: We need to rid ourselves of adultery and hatred (see Matt. 5:21-22,28); we need to add wisdom and knowledge (see Col. 2:3).

4. Call on quads to read and comment on their lists. Place one on the Transformed From Wall and the other on the Transformed To Wall.

5. Ask a volunteer to pray that God will cleanse members of your group and church.

**Stimulating One Another to Love and Good Deeds (20 minutes)**

1. Read Hebrews 10:24 from your session segment poster.

2. Invite volunteers to share testimonies of what God has done this week in their lives that has been meaningful, challenging, or instructive.

3. Encourage members to share questions or concerns they have written for consideration. As time permits, guide the group in answering the questions.

4. As time permits, discuss one or more of the following questions:

• In God's sight, is your inner or outer being more important? Why?

• What are some of the ways Jesus expressed positive and negative emotions?

• How can negative emotions be expressed in acceptable ways?

• In what ways are you able to express love like that described in 1 Corinthians 13? Give an example.

• Are emotional impulses wrong? Why or why not? How can a believer develop control for emotional impulses? What is your role? What is God's role?

5. Ask members to turn to page 130 and share their responses to the third activity.

**Preparing the Bride for Her Bridegroom (5 minutes)**

1. Call on a person to read Matthew 24:36-51. Ask members to listen for ways the bride (church) needs to prepare for the return of Christ.

2. As time permits, ask and discuss these questions:

• Since we do not know the day or hour of Christ's return, how should we live our lives?

• What cleansing, purifying, or preparation is needed in our church?

• How can we apply this Scripture to our lives, families, and church?

3. Call on one member to pray for your church to continue to prepare for the Lord's return.

**Praying for One Another (10 minutes)**

1. (Quads) Read James 5:16 from your session segment poster. Ask members to share personal, family, church, or work-related prayer requests that primarily focus on developing the mind of Christ or purifying the bride.

2. (Quads) Ask quads to pray specifically for one another for forgiveness, healing, encouragement, guidance, wisdom, knowledge, understanding, courage, strength, faithfulness, or for specific requests.

**Closing the Session (5 minutes)**

1. Invite members to share questions or concerns that came up during the session that the group should remember in prayer.

2. Preview unit 9. Ask members to pay special attention this week to ways they relate to things and people.

3. Close by praying that God will guide and instruct members in a right way of relating to people and things, reserving their supreme love for God alone.

**AFTER THE SESSION**

❏ Read and complete the evaluations and activities described in the Standard After the Session instructions (p. 18 LG).

# JESUS' RELATIONS

---

## SESSION GOALS

This session will help members understand Jesus' teachings on materialism and the ways He related to people. Members will demonstrate determination to lay up treasures in heaven and to live like Christ in their relationship to people.

---

### BEFORE THE SESSION

❏ Read and complete the activities in the Standard Before the Session instructions (p. 17 LG).

❏ Pay special attention to what God may be doing in your own life. Your model of responsiveness may do more to help others develop the mind of Christ than all the words you say. If God leads you to make some major adjustments in your lifestyle, obey Him.

### DURING THE SESSION

### Hearing What the Spirit Is Saying (as members arrive)

1. (Individuals) Ask members to review what God has been saying to them during the study of unit 9. Ask them to identify a Scripture and a name of Christ that have been meaningful this week. Then ask them to identify and mark the issue or subject in which God seems to be working most actively to develop the mind of Christ. These will be shared later in the session.

2. (Individuals) Ask members to write out any questions for which they would like to find answers.

### Magnifying the Lord and Exalting His Name (5 minutes)

1. Open the session by asking God to reveal every relationship to people or things that does not reflect a Christlike quality. Encourage members to pray as they feel led to worship God for who He is and acknowledge Him for what He has done. Encourage them to use the names of Christ to exalt His name together in prayer.

2. After prayer, invite members to share ways God revealed Himself this week through His names. Ask: Which name of Christ has been most meaningful to you and why?

### Transforming by the Word (15 minutes)

1. (Pairs) Ask members to pair up and quote this week's memory verse, Matthew 6:20-21. Then, as time permits, ask them to alternate quoting verses from previous units. Encourage them to use their Scripture memory cards as a reference.

2. Ask members to share what God said to them through this week's memory verse or other Scripture that has been meaningful.

3. (Quads—two groups) Distribute poster board or newsprint and markers to each of two quads. Ask members to help you make two lists related to our relationship with people and things. Focus on this unit's Scriptures only. Ask one quad to make a list of things, actions, or attitudes identified or implied in Scriptures during unit 9 that need to be *cleansed from* one's mind and life. Ask the second quad to make a list of things, actions, or attitudes identified or implied in Scriptures in unit 9 that need to be *incorporated into* one's mind and life. For example: We do not need to worry over food and clothes; we do need to seek the Kingdom above all else (see Matt. 6:30-33).

4. Call on quads to read and comment on their lists. Place one on the Transformed From Wall and the other on the Transformed To Wall.

5. Ask a volunteer to pray that God will cleanse members of your group and church.

**Stimulating One Another to Love and Good Deeds (20 minutes)**

1. Ask someone to quote Hebrews 10:24.

2. Invite volunteers to share testimonies of what God has done this week in their lives that has been meaningful, challenging, or instructive.

3. Encourage members to state questions or concerns they have written for consideration. As time permits, guide the group in answering the questions.

4. Ask members to turn to page 133. Ask volunteers to share their response to the second activity. Was there anything in the activity on pages 133-134 that God has indicated you must get rid of? What? Have you obeyed Him?

5. Now ask members to turn to page 134 and share their responses, if any, to the last activity.

6. Ask members to turn to page 139 and share their responses to the activity which rated your Friend-friend relationship with Christ.

7. As time permits, discuss one or more of the following questions:

- If greed is idolatry, how does God view the way many Christians love the world and the things of the world?

- What are some ways God has been your Provider? (see pp. 133-134).

- What can you do to be more single-minded rather than double-minded?

- How does the way a person treats other people reflect or fail to reflect the mind of Christ?

**Preparing the Bride for Her Bridegroom (5 minutes)**

1. Call on a person to read Revelation 2:1-18. Ask members to listen for ways the bride (church) may need to repent and return to Christ.

2. As time permits, ask and discuss these questions:

- What in these messages of Christ to His churches applies to our church?

- How can our church repent and return in these areas?

- What cleansing, purifying, or preparation is needed in our church?

- How can we apply this Scripture to our lives, families, and church?

3. Call on one member to pray for your church to continue to prepare for the Lord's return.

**Praying for One Another (10 minutes)**

1. (Quads) Read James 5:16 from your session segment poster and ask members to share personal, family, church, or work-related prayer requests that primarily focus on developing the mind of Christ or purifying the bride.

2. (Quads) Ask quads to pray specifically for one another for forgiveness, healing, encouragement, guidance, wisdom, knowledge, understanding, courage, strength, faithfulness, or for specific requests.

**Closing the Session (5 minutes)**

1. Invite members to share questions or concerns that came up during the session that the group should remember in prayer.

2. Preview unit 10. Encourage each group member to pay special attention to his or her relationship to the Father and Holy Spirit.

3. Close by praying that God will teach and enable members to live in the fullness of the Spirit.

**AFTER THE SESSION**

❑ Read and complete the evaluations and activities described in the Standard After the Session instructions (p. 18 LG).

❑ Is God leading you to take actions that you have not responded to because you think "But I am the teacher"? Do you need to obey Him in an area of giving that would be a model for the members of your group? (Don't respond because it would be a nice thing to do; respond because God is leading you.)

❑ Prepare to share ways you plan to use *The Mind of Christ Worship Video Series* on the crucifixion (related to unit 11) and resurrection (related to unit 12). See pages 7-8 LG for further instructions. Since these require one hour or more each, plan for additional sessions if necessary.

# GROUP SESSION 10

# LIVING IN THE SPIRIT

## SESSION GOALS

This session will help members understand ways they can practice living in the Spirit. Members will demonstrate a desire to know and do the will of their Heavenly Father.

**BEFORE THE SESSION**

❏ Read and complete the activities in the Standard Before the Session instructions (p. 17 LG).

❏ Finalize plans for showing *The Mind of Christ Worship Video Series.* If you have not done so, read "After the Session" for session 9. Be prepared to share specifics about when and where the videos will be shown.

❏ Be prepared to identify resources available in the church media library related to the crucifixion and resurrection.

**DURING THE SESSION**

**Hearing What the Spirit Is Saying (as members arrive)**

1. (Individuals) Ask members to review what God has been saying to them during the study of unit 10. Ask them to identify a Scripture and a name of Christ that have been meaningful this week. Then ask them to identify and mark the issue or subject in which God seems to be working most actively to develop the mind of Christ. These will be shared later in the session.

2. (Individuals) Ask members to write out any questions for which they would like to find answers.

**Magnifying the Lord and Exalting His Name (5 minutes)**

1. Open the session by asking God to fill members with His Holy Spirit and enable them to experience abundant life in Christ. Encourage members to pray as they feel led to worship, praise, or thank God for who

He is and what He has done. Encourage them to use the names of Christ to exalt His name together in prayer.

2. After prayer, invite members to share ways God revealed Himself this week through His names. Ask: Which name of Christ has been most meaningful to you and why?

**Transforming by the Word (15 minutes)**

1. (Pairs) Ask members to pair up and quote this week's memory verse, John 6:63. Then, as time permits, ask them to alternate quoting verses from previous units. Encourage them to use their Scripture memory cards as a reference.

2. Ask members to share what God said to them through this week's memory verse or other Scripture that has been meaningful.

3. (Quads—two groups) Distribute poster board or newsprint and markers to each of two quads. Ask members to help you make two lists related to living in the flesh versus living in the Spirit. Focus on this unit's Scriptures only. Ask one quad to make a list of things, actions, or attitudes identified or implied in Scriptures during unit 10 that need to be *cleansed from* one's mind and life. Ask the second quad to make a list of things, actions, or attitudes identified or implied in Scriptures in unit 10 that need to be *incorporated into* one's mind and life. For example: We need to eliminate being drunk with wine and add being filled with the Spirit (see Eph. 5:18).

4. Call on quads to read and comment on their lists. Place one on the Transformed From Wall and the other on the Transformed To Wall.

5. Ask a volunteer to pray that God will cleanse members of your group and church.

**Stimulating One Another to Love and Good Deeds (20 minutes)**

1. Read Hebrews 10:24 from your session segment poster.

2. Invite volunteers to share testimonies of what God has done this week in their lives that has been meaningful, challenging, or instructive.

3. Encourage members to state questions or concerns they have written for consideration. As time permits, guide the group in answering the questions.

4. Ask members to turn to page 143. Ask volunteers to share their responses to second and third activities.

5. As time permits, discuss one or more of the following questions:

• What are some of the differences in living in the ways of the world and living in the Spirit?

• What are some areas of your life where God has revealed that the material world has too much influence in your life and decision making?

• If you were to write a purpose statement for your life, what would it say? How well does it blend with or conflict with the purpose statements of Jesus? (see p. 147)

• What have you learned about life from the ways Jesus related to His Father and the Holy Spirit? How should you relate to the Father and the Spirit?

**Preparing the Bride for Her Bridegroom (5 minutes)**

1. Call on a person to read Revelation 2:19-29. Ask members to listen for ways the bride (church) may need to repent and return to the Lord.

2. As time permits, ask and discuss these questions:

• What in these messages of Christ to His churches applies to our church?

• What cleansing, purifying, or preparation is needed in our church?

• How can we apply this Scripture to our lives, families, and church?

3. Call on one member to pray for your church to continue to prepare for the Lord's return.

**Praying for One Another (10 minutes)**

1. (Quads) Read James 5:16 from your session segment poster and ask members to share personal, family, church, or work-related prayer requests that primarily focus on developing the mind of Christ or purifying the bride.

2. (Quads) Ask quads to pray specifically for one another for forgiveness, healing, encouragement, guidance, wisdom, knowledge, understanding, courage, strength, faithfulness, or for specific requests.

**Closing the Session (5 minutes)**

1. Invite members to share questions or concerns that came up during the session that the group should remember in prayer.

2. Preview unit 11. If you are planning one or more sessions related to the crucifixion (unit 11) or the resurrection (unit 12) using *The Mind of Christ Worship Video Series,* discuss plans with the group. Identify resources that are available in the church media library that relate to these two events in the life of Christ that members may want to use in conjunction with the next two units.

3. Close by praying that God will clearly reveal the nature of His holiness and love that was demonstrated by Christ on the cross.

**AFTER THE SESSION**

❏ Read and complete the evaluations and activities described in the Standard After the Session instructions (p. 18 LG).

❏ Finalize plans for viewing *The Mind of Christ Worship Video Series.*

# HOLINESS AND LOVE

---

### SESSION GOALS

This session will help members understand the nature of Christ's holiness and love. Members will demonstrate a desire to exemplify Christ's love in their lives.

---

**BEFORE THE SESSION**

❏ Read and complete the activities in the Standard Before the Session instructions (p. 17 LG).

❏ If you have not done so already, prepare a poster or copy of the Scripture on p. 4 LG and display it for use in this session.

❏ Prepare to share plans for viewing *The Mind of Christ Worship Video Series.*

**DURING THE SESSION**

### Hearing What the Spirit Is Saying (as members arrive)

1. (Individuals) Ask members to review what God has been saying to them during the study of unit 11. Ask them to identify a Scripture and a name of Christ that have been meaningful this week. Then ask them to identify and mark the issue or subject in which God seems to be working most actively to develop the mind of Christ. These will be shared later in the session.

2. (Individuals) Ask members to write out any questions for which they would like to find answers.

### Magnifying the Lord and Exalting His Name (5 minutes)

1. Open the session with prayer, asking God to convince every member of His holiness and unconditional love demonstrated on the cross. Encourage members to pray as they feel led to worship God for who He is and acknowledge Him for what He has done. Encourage them to use the names of Christ to exalt His name together in prayer.

2. After prayer, invite members to share ways God revealed Himself this week through His names. Ask: Which name of Christ has been most meaningful to you and why?

### Transforming by the Word (15 minutes)

1. (Pairs) Ask members to pair up and quote this week's memory verses, 1 Peter 1:15-16. Then, as time permits, ask them to alternate quoting verses from previous units. Encourage them to use their Scripture memory cards as a reference.

2. Ask members to share what God said to them through this week's memory verses or other Scripture that has been meaningful.

3. (Quads—two groups) Distribute poster board or newsprint and markers to each of two quads. Ask members to help you make two lists related to holiness and love. Focus on this unit's Scriptures only. Ask one quad to make a list of things, actions, or attitudes identified or implied in Scriptures during unit 11 that need to be *cleansed from* one's mind and life. Ask the second quad to make a list of things, actions, or attitudes identified or implied in Scriptures in unit 11 that need to be *incorporated into* one's mind and life. For example: We need to rid ourselves of the filthiness of the flesh and strive to perfect our holiness (see 2 Cor. 7:1).

4. Call on quads to read and comment on their lists. Place one on the Transformed From Wall and the other on the Transformed To Wall.

5. Ask a volunteer to pray that God will cleanse members of your group and church.

## Stimulating One Another to Love and Good Deeds (20 minutes)

1. Read Hebrews 10:24.

2. Invite volunteers to share testimonies of what God has done this week in their lives that has been meaningful, challenging, or instructive.

3. Encourage members to state questions or concerns they have written for consideration. As time permits, guide the group in answering the questions.

4. Read John 13:1 from the poster (p. 4 LG). Ask: If Christ loved us enough to die for us on the cross, how should we respond to Him? to each other?

5. As time permits, discuss one or more of the following questions:

- How can God be both loving and holy? How are the two related?

- How would you define *holiness?* What are some ways Jesus demonstrated holiness? How can we demonstrate holiness? Where does our holiness come from?

- How do you define *love?* What are some ways Jesus demonstrated love? How can we demonstrate love?

## Preparing the Bride for Her Bridegroom (5 minutes)

1. Call on a person to read Revelation 3:1-22. Ask members to listen for ways the bride (church) may need to repent and return to the Lord.

2. As time permits, ask and discuss these questions:

- What in these messages of Christ to His churches applies to our church? How do we need to respond?

- What cleansing, purifying, or preparation is needed in our church?

- How can we apply this Scripture to our lives, families, and church?

3. Call on one member to pray for your church to continue to prepare for the Lord's return.

## Praying for One Another (10 minutes)

1. (Quads) Read James 5:16 from your session segment poster and ask members to share personal, family, church, or work-related prayer requests that primarily focus on developing the mind of Christ or purifying the bride.

2. (Quads) Ask quads to pray specifically for one another for forgiveness, healing, encouragement, guidance, wisdom, knowledge, understanding, courage, strength, faithfulness, or for specific requests.

## Closing the Session (5 minutes)

1. Invite members to share questions or concerns that came up during the session that the group should remember in prayer.

2. Preview unit 12. Remind members of additional sessions related to viewing the videos on the crucifixion or resurrection. Mention once again the resources available in the church media library related to these two events.

3. Ask members to prepare a brief written evaluation of the small-group study of *The Mind of Christ.* Encourage them to share any suggestions they may have to improve the experience for group members in future studies. Announce that these will be received during the next session.

4. Close by praying that God will magnify and exalt His Son Jesus in the minds and hearts of members this week.

### AFTER THE SESSION

❏ Read and complete the evaluations and activities described in the Standard After the Session instructions (p. 18 LG).

❏ Who is the person in your church responsible for discipleship training? Find out from him or her when another small-group study of *The Mind of Christ* will be offered. Ask what other approaches to the study of *The Mind of Christ* will be offered in the future. Also find out what future training opportunities have been scheduled so you can share this information with your group in the session.

# GROUP SESSION 12
# EXALTING CHRIST

---

## SESSION GOALS

This session will help members understand the names and offices of Christ. Members will demonstrate a commitment to an ongoing process of developing the mind of Christ.

---

**BEFORE THE SESSION**

❏ Read and complete the activities in the Standard Before the Session instructions (p. 17 LG).

❏ Prepare a sheet or poster listing information about upcoming discipleship training opportunities in your church. See unit 11 "After the Session."

❏ If you plan to give out copies of Philippians 2:5-11, secure those before the session.

**DURING THE SESSION**

**Hearing What the Spirit Is Saying (as members arrive)**

1. (Individuals) Ask members to review what God has been saying to them during the study of unit 12. Ask them to identify a Scripture and a name of Christ that have been meaningful this week. Then ask them to identify and mark the issue or subject in which God seems to be working most actively to develop the mind of Christ. These will be shared later in the session.

2. (Individuals) Ask members to write out any questions for which they would like to find answers.

3. If members have prepared an evaluation of the study, take up the evaluations. If they have not prepared their evaluations, encourage them to take a few moments to write down their comments or suggestions.

**Magnifying the Lord and Exalting His Name (5 minutes)**

1. Open the session by asking God to exalt His Son Jesus in your hearts and minds. Ask God to exalt His

Son through your church in your community. Encourage members to pray as they feel led to worship God for who He is and acknowledge Him for what He has done. Encourage them to use the names of Christ to exalt His name together in prayer.

2. After prayer, invite members to share ways God revealed Himself this week through His names. Ask: Which name of Christ has been most meaningful to you and why?

**Transforming by the Word (15 minutes)**

1. (Pairs) Ask members to pair up and quote this week's memory verse, Colossians 1:18. Then, as time permits, ask them to alternate quoting verses from previous units. Encourage them to use their Scripture memory cards as a reference.

2. Ask members to share what God said to them through this week's memory verse or other Scripture that has been meaningful.

3. Ask group members to identify some of the attitudes, actions, or things that God has removed from their minds and lives during this study.

4. Ask members to describe attitudes, actions, virtues, and thoughts that God has added to their minds and lives during this study.

5. Take time as a group to thank God for what He has been doing to cleanse group members and your church. Ask God to continue to shape members into the image of His Son Jesus.

**Stimulating One Another to Love and Good Deeds (20 minutes)**

1. Lead the group in quoting Hebrews 10:24.

2. Invite volunteers to share testimonies of what God has done this week in their lives that has been meaningful, challenging, or instructive.

3. Encourage members to state questions or concerns they have written for consideration. As time permits, guide the group in answering the questions.

4. Distribute the sheet or point to the poster with upcoming discipleship training opportunities. Encourage members to participate in one of these courses in order to continue their growth as disciples. Mention that some may want to participate in the next study of *The Mind of Christ* as a means of review and continued growth.

5. As time permits, discuss one or more of the following questions:

- What are some reasons we should worship Christ because of His offices of Prophet, Priest, and King? How can we worship Him?

- Where will the greatest battles for having the mind of Christ be fought? What spiritual weapons and armor are available to you? What is your source of victory?

- What is the most significant thing God has done in your life during the past 12 weeks?

- How have other members of the body helped you become more of what God wants you to be?

- What do you sense God is doing to prepare your church for His Son's return?

- What do you sense God wants you to do next on your pilgrimage in developing the mind of Christ?

**Preparing the Bride for Her Bridegroom (5 minutes)**

1. Call on a person to read Revelation 22:1-21. Ask members to listen for ways the bride (church) needs to prepare for the return of Christ.

2. As time permits, ask and discuss these questions:

- What is the message of the bride in the last days? (v. 17)

- What has God been saying to you or doing in your life related to the return of His Son?

- What preparations have you seen our church making in purifying herself to prepare us for the marriage of the Lamb?

- What cleansing, purifying, or preparation is still needed in our church?

- How can we apply this Scripture to our lives, families, and church?

3. Call on one member to pray thanking God for the progress in purity these past weeks and asking God to continue His refining work.

**Praying for One Another (10 minutes)**

1. (Quads) Ask members to identify one area of their lives or minds that needs special attention. Ask each member to share (one person at a time) a way the quad can pray for him or her. Once a person has shared a request, let the quad pray for that request. Then repeat the process for each person, one at a time.

**Closing the Session (5 minutes)**

1. (Optional) Give members a copy of Philippians 2:5-11. Suggest they display it in their homes as a reminder of the work God is doing in their lives to develop the mind of Christ.

2. Ask members to fill in the Church Study Course form in the back of their books (p. 223). Provide guidance for those who have not previously participated in the Church Study Course. Explain that members will receive a diploma as a symbol of the work invested in this study. Tell members about the video and audio approaches to *The Mind of Christ* and suggest they may want to participate in one of these. A diploma also is available for each of these approaches.

**AFTER THE SESSION**

❏ Read and complete the evaluations and activities described in the Standard After the Session instructions (p. 18 LG).

❏ Complete the Church Study Course forms, sign and mail them to Church Study Course Resources Section; 127 Ninth Avenue, North; Nashville, TN 37234. When your church receives the diplomas, you and the pastor need to sign them. Plan for an appropriate time to award the diplomas to the small-group participants.

❏ Are any members in your group qualified and spiritually gifted to lead a future study of *The Mind of Christ*? If so, give their names to the discipleship director for possible use in future groups.

❏ Gather the six session segment posters and the headings for the Transformed To and Transformed From walls. Keep them for use in a future study of *The Mind of Christ*.

❏ If you received written evaluations from group members, take time to review their comments and suggestions for future small-group studies of *The Mind of Christ*.

❏ Take some time to evaluate your group study of *The Mind of Christ*. Use the following questions to start your thinking. Make notes for yourself on separate paper or in your journal. Begin this time with a prayer for God's perspective.

• How has God used this course and small-group study to influence or improve my relationship with Him?

• What personal progress have I made in developing the mind of Christ?

• Did I reflect the mind and behavior of Christ as I led this study? If not, what are some ways I can improve if I lead the study again?

• What changes have I observed in the lives of group members? Have other people observed these changes also?

• What was the most meaningful experience for the group in the study?

• What would I do differently in a future study of the course? Consider enlistment of members, size of group, meeting time and place, schedule, learning activities, prayer times, and so forth.

• What shall I do next in my service or growth in discipleship? Shall I lead another group through *The Mind of Christ*? Should I participate in one of the other discipleship training courses?

❏ Conclude your time in prayer. Thank God for all He has done in your life and the lives of group members. Thank Him for His Son Jesus and the love He has shown to you through Christ. Take time to pray specifically for the continued spiritual growth of each member of your group.

# MASTERS FOR ADDITIONAL VISUAL SUPPORT

The following masters can be used for making overhead transparencies or reproduced for handouts for use with *The Mind of Christ* resources. Group leaders, conference facilitators, pastors, and other church staff members can use some or all of these for overviewing, reviewing, or discussing *The Mind of Christ*. They also can be used with the LIFE course.

Before using these masters, read pages 6-8 LG (Offering a Study of The Mind of Christ) and pages 19-21 LG (Introductory Session). Study the corresponding section (in parentheses) in *The Mind of Christ Member's Book* so you can explain details or answer questions.

### Introducing the LIFE Course

The first five masters are for use in the Introductory Session of the LIFE course.

MASTER 1: THE MIND OF CHRIST, Philippians 2:5-11 (pp. 17-20)

MASTER 2: SIX CHARACTERISTICS OF THE CHRISTLIKE MIND (pp. 12-17)

MASTER 3: THREE STAGES IN DEVELOPING THE MIND OF CHRIST (pp. 20-26)

MASTER 4: CONFORMING TO THE IMAGE OF CHRIST (all)

MASTER 5: THE MIND OF CHRIST UNIT OVERVIEWS (all)

### Overheads for Conference Settings

The remaining overhead transparencies can be used in settings where you overview, discuss, or review content. By studying the corresponding sections in the LIFE course, you will be prepared to elaborate on each of these areas.

You can also use these remaining masters with the LIFE course. Participants have this information in the *Member's Book,* so the best way to use these masters is

to have them enlarged to poster size for use in the small groups.

MASTER 6: FREEDOM IN CHRIST (units 2-3). This master can be used to explain to members the importance of making lists and allowing Christ to set them free from the bondage to sin. You could even help people begin making some of these lists.

MASTER 7: SEVENTEEN VIRTUES OF THE MIND OF CHRIST (units 4-5). This master can be used to review or discuss the contrasts between the Christlike virtues, their opposites and perversions.

MASTER 8: CHARACTERISTICS OF THE SERVANT MIND (pp. 93-104, 197-198). This master can be used to focus attention on the characteristics of servanthood and to explain their meaning more fully.

MASTER 9: FIRST FOUR BEATITUDES (pp. 106-111, 203-209) and MASTER 10: SECOND FOUR BEATITUDES (pp. 111-112, 210-217). These two masters show the relationship between the first four and the second four Beatitudes. Discuss the meaning and the ways God uses circumstances to develop these attitudes in a believer.

MASTER 11: BEHAVIORS OF CHRISTLIKE LOVE (pp. 151-157, 180-181). This master reminds people of the behaviors of Christlike love. Suggest practical ways to exhibit each of these behaviors.

### Scripture Master

The two Scripture passages (Hebrews 10:24 and Philippians 2:5-11) on pages 60-61 LG can be photocopied for members or use around the church. Ideas for their use in the LIFE course can be found on page 15 LG.

# THE MIND OF CHRIST
## PHILIPPIANS 2:5-11

## Part 1: Christ's Freedom

"Let this mind be in you, which was also in Christ Jesus" (v. 5).

## Part 2: Christ's Lifestyle

"Who, being in the form of God, thought it not robbery to be equal with God" (v. 6).

## Part 3: Christ's Servanthood

"But made himself of no reputation, and took upon him the form of a servant" (v. 7).

## Part 4: Christ's Humanity

"And was made in the likeness of men: And being found in fashion as a man" (vv. 7-8).

## Part 5: Christ's Holiness and Love

"He humbled himself, and became obedient unto death, even the death of the cross" (v. 8).

## Part 6: Christ's Name

"Wherefore God also hath exalted him, and given him a name which is above every name: That at the name of Jesus every knee should bow, of things in heaven, and things in earth, and things under the earth; And that every tongue should confess that Jesus Christ is Lord, to the glory of God the Father" (vv. 9-11).

# SIX CHARACTERISTICS
# OF THE CHRISTLIKE MIND

## ALIVE

"The mind set on the Spirit is life and peace" (Rom. 8:6, NASB).

## SINGLE-MINDED

"I am afraid, lest . . . your minds should be led astray from the simplicity and purity of devotion to Christ" (2 Cor. 11:3, NASB).

## LOWLY

"In lowliness of mind let each esteem other better than than themselves" (Phil. 2:3).

## PURE

"Unto the pure all things are pure: but unto them that are defiled and unbelieving is nothing pure; but even their mind and conscience is defiled" (Titus 1:15).

## RESPONSIVE

"He opened their minds to understand the Scriptures" (Luke 24:45, NASB).

## PEACEFUL

"The mind set on the Spirit is life and peace" (Rom. 8:6, NASB).

Master 2, *The Mind of Christ* © 1994, LifeWay Press.

You have permission to reproduce and use with *The Mind of Christ* resources.

# THREE STAGES IN DEVELOPING THE MIND OF CHRIST

1. **Beginning: The Will Principle**
   *Set* your mind on things above.


2. **Growing: The River Principle**
   Allow God to *renew* your mind.


3. **Qualified: The Readiness Principle**
   *Gird up* your mind for action.

# CONFORMING TO THE IMAGE OF CHRIST

- The virtues of godly wisdom (James 3:17)

- The fruit of the Spirit (Galatians 5:22-23)

- The characteristics of the servant mind

- The qualities described in the Beatitudes (Matthew 5:3-10)

- The model of Christ in expressing emotions

- The model of Christ in relationship to things and people

- The model of Christ in relationship to the Father and the Holy Spirit

- The model of Christ's use of the Scriptures and prayer

- The character and behavior of holiness

- The actions of Christlike love

# THE MIND OF CHRIST UNIT OVERVIEWS

**UNIT 1:** You will understand a three-stage process through which God will guide you. You will understand six characteristics of a Christlike mind.

**UNITS 2-3:** You will begin a process through which God will begin His work of setting you free from the bondage to sin.

**UNITS 4-5:** You will understand 17 virtues of the mind of Christ. God will be working to develop those virtues in your life.

**UNIT 6:** You will understand the importance of servanthood, following the example of Christ. God will be working to develop in your life the characteristics of servanthood.

**UNITS 7-10:** You will focus on Christ's humanity by studying the Beatitudes, the emotions of Christ, Christ's relationships, and living in the Spirit. God will be working to purify your mind and life to reflect the perfect humanity of Christ.

**UNIT 11:** You will understand how love and holiness work together and enhance each other. God will be working in you to make you holy and teach you to love with a Christlike love.

**UNIT 12:** You will understand how God has exalted Christ through His names. You will be challenged to bow your knees by surrendering to the absolute lordship of Christ in your life.

# FREEDOM IN CHRIST

"It was for freedom that Christ set us free;
therefore keep standing firm and do not be subject
again to a yoke of slavery" (Gal. 5:1, NASB).

| God's goals are to move your… | from… | to… |
|---|---|---|
| lusts | being self-seeking | seeking the Kingdom |
| habits | being careless | being Spirit controlled |
| loyalties | being scattered | being prayerful |
| relationships | serving self | serving God |
| prejudices | being accidental | being scriptural |
| ambitions | honoring self | honoring God |
| duties | compulsion | eternity |
| debts | temporal ones | eternal ones |
| possessions | ownership | stewardship |
| fears | being self-protective | finding security in Christ |
| weaknesses | being tools of Satan | being tools of God |
| hurts | producing resentment | producing love |

Master 6, *The Mind of Christ* © 1994, LifeWay Press.

You have permission to reproduce and use with *The Mind of Christ* resources.

# SEVENTEEN VIRTUES OF THE MIND OF CHRIST

| Eight Virtues of Godly Wisdom | | |
|---|---|---|
| **Opposite** | **Christlike Virtue** | **Perversion** |
| Lustful | *Pure* | Puritanical |
| Fussy | *Peaceable* | Compromising |
| Harsh | *Gentle* | Unkind restraint |
| Unapproachable | *Entreatable* | Yes-person |
| Merciless | *Merciful* | Indulgent |
| Fruitless | *Fruitful* | Fruit-obsessed |
| Wavering | *Steadfast* | Inflexible |
| Lying | *Honest* | Brutal |

| Nine Fruit of the Spirit | | |
|---|---|---|
| **Opposite** | **Christlike Virtue** | **Perversion** |
| Hate, Fear | *Love* | Possessive, Permissive |
| Pain | *Joy* | Frenzy |
| War | *Peace* | Neutral |
| Impatient | *Longsuffering* | Lenient |
| Hard | *Gentleness* | Soft |
| Badness | *Goodness* | Finicky Nice |
| Unbelief | *Faith* | Presumption |
| Arrogance | *Meekness* | Weakness |
| Undisciplined | *Temperance* | Fleshly Effort |

# CHARACTERISTICS OF THE SERVANT MIND

Humble

Obedient

Willing

Loyal

Faithful

Watchful

Courageous

Not Quarrelsome

Gentle

Able to Teach

Patient

Meek

Good

Wise

Master 8, *The Mind of Christ* © 1994, LifeWay Press.

You have permission to reproduce and use with *The Mind of Christ* resources.

# FIRST FOUR BEATITUDES
## (MATT. 5:3-6)

1. Blessed are the poor in spirit: for theirs is the kingdom of heaven.

2. Blessed are they that mourn: for they shall be comforted.

3. Blessed are the meek: for they shall inherit the earth.

4. Blessed are they which do hunger and thirst after righteousness: for they shall be filled.

| | |
|---|---|
| Poor in Spirit.................................Principle of Need | |
| Mourn...........................................Principle of Brokenness | |
| Meek..............................................Principle of Submission | |
| Hungry ..........................................Principle of Yearning | |

- **Basis for Happiness:** Your need

- **Keys** to God's Heart

- **Focus:** Turn your mind toward God. You learn about God. You learn that God is God.

- **Command:** Love God—"Thou shalt love the Lord thy God with all thy heart, and with all thy soul, and with all thy mind, and with all thy strength" (Mark 12:30).

- **Object:** God gives according to your need to mold and shape you into the image of Christ. He equips you with the character of Christ.

- **Door to Greatness**

- **Worship:** Lower Levels of Worship—Praise to God comes out of your need and His sufficiency to meet your need.

# SECOND FOUR BEATITUDES
# (MATT. 5:7-11)

5. Blessed are the merciful: for they shall obtain mercy.

6. Blessed are the pure in heart: for they shall see God.

7. Blessed are the peacemakers: for they shall be called the children of God.

8. Blessed are they which are persecuted for righteousness' sake: for theirs is the kingdom of heaven. Blessed are ye, when men shall revile you, and persecute you, and shall say all manner of evil against you falsely, for my sake. Rejoice, and be exceeding glad: for great is your reward in heaven: for so persecuted they the prophets which were before you.

| | |
|---|---|
| Merciful | Principle of Reciprocity |
| Pure in Heart | Principle of Perfect Heart |
| Peacemakers | Principle of Reconciliation |
| Persecuted | Principle of Identification |

• **Basis for Happiness:** Your giving

• **Keys** to Christ's Character

• **Focus:** Turn your mind toward others. You serve in Christ's spirit. You reflect Christ to a watching world.

• **Command:** Love Others—"Thou shalt love thy neighbor as thyself" (Mark 12:31).

• **Object:** God works through you to reveal Himself to a watching world. You become identified with Christ as you reveal His character to others.

• **Practice of Greatness**

• **Worship:** Higher Levels of Worship—Praise to God comes from the exercise of your character as you reveal the character of Christ to others.

# BEHAVIORS OF CHRISTLIKE LOVE

| Love | Holiness |
|------|----------|
| Suffers long | Holy Relationships |
| Is kind | Holy Purposes |
| Does not envy | Holy Heart |
| Does not brag | Holy Speech |
| Is not arrogant | Holy Service |
| Does not act unbecomingly | Holy Behavior |
| Does not seek its own | Holy Desires |
| Is not provoked | Holy Temperament |
| Does not take into account a wrong | Holy Bookkeeping |
| Does not rejoice in unrighteousness | Holy Conscience |
| Rejoices in the truth | Holy Mind |
| Bears all things | Holy Stability |
| Believes all things | Holy Values |
| Hopes all things | Holy Expectations |
| Endures all things | Holy Sacrifice |

*Let us consider how to stimulate one another to love and good deeds.*

*—Hebrews 10:24, NASB*

# The Mind of Christ

Let this mind be in you, which was also in Christ Jesus: Who, being in the form of God, thought it not robbery to be equal with God: But made himself of no reputation, and took upon him the form of a servant, and was made in the likeness of men: And being found in fashion as a man, he humbled himself, and became obedient unto death, even the death of the cross. Wherefore God also hath highly exalted him, and given him a name which is above every name: That at the name of Jesus every knee should bow. . . . And that every tongue should confess that Jesus Christ is Lord, to the glory of God the Father.

—Philippians 2:5-11

# THE MIND
## OF
# CHRIST

### LIFE COURSE

"Let this mind be in you, which was also
in Christ Jesus ... (Phil. 2:5).

Join us for an introduction to T. W. Hunt's acclaimed study
on developing the mind of Christ.

You will be provided complete information on what this
12-week course can do for your spiritual development. At
the end of the introductory session, you can decide
whether to participate at this time.

A book fee of $_____ will be required of each participant.

Date: _____

Time: _____

Location: _____

# THE MIND OF CHRIST

## VIDEO CONFERENCE SERIES

"Let this mind be in you, which was also
in Christ Jesus . . . (Phil. 2:5).

Experience T. W. Hunt's acclaimed study on developing the
mind of Christ. Join Dr. Hunt in a video conference setting
as he shares his personal spiritual experiences.

|  | Date | Time |
|---|---|---|
| Christ's Freedom | _____ | _____ |
| Christ's Lifestyle | _____ | _____ |
| Christ's Servanthood | _____ | _____ |
| Christ's Humanity | _____ | _____ |
| Christ's Holiness and Love | _____ | _____ |
| Christ's Name | _____ | _____ |

Location: _____

# THE MIND OF CHRIST

## WORSHIP VIDEO SERIES

"Let this mind be in you, which
was also in Christ Jesus . . . (Phil. 2:5).

Join T. W. Hunt as he details Christ's experiences during
the crucifixion and resurrection. These two messages will
offer insight into what Christ did for your salvation.

The Crucifixion

Date: _____

Time: _____

Location: _____


The Resurrection

Date: _____

Time: _____

Location: _____

Promotion Master 3, *The Mind of Christ* © 1994, LifeWay Press.

You have permission to reproduce and use with *The Mind of Christ* resources.